Defining **Moments**

A Suburban Father's Journey

into his Son's Oxy Addiction

By Bradley V. DeHaven

Dedication

I dedicate this book to my wife Lisa, the one person who has been with me through more ups and downs than anyone could ever imagine. You never know when or if the perfect person will appear. The fateful night I set eyes on her set in motion everything that would happen to me for the rest of my life. I couldn't be happier that I was fortunate enough to be in the right place at the perfect time to meet my soul mate. She is the most beautiful person, both inside and out. She has been an inspiration for mc and making her happy is the goal of my life. We are best friends, confidants, partners, and true lovers and together we are one. I can't imagine my existence without her, and I know that everything I am and all I will become is shaped by her genuine kindness. Meeting Lisa is the most important defining moment in my life.

Table of Contents

Acknowledgments

I would like to thank all of the drug and alcohol rehabilitation professionals who choose to tackle the daunting task of attempting to help those in this world who cannot take just one drink but must consume the whole bottle, and those who cannot take a prescription pill as prescribed, but must crush, snort, smoke or inject these powerful drugs to feed the monster of addiction. Many of these counselors and staff who help the addicts in our lives were once addicts themselves. They choose to "give back" because they have either finally come to understand what caused them to want to destroy themselves and are compelled to share this knowledge, or they know that they can only continue their sobriety by staying where they found it, or both. Either way, they are the students who became the teachers of recovery and only they are bullet proof to the lies that flow so freely from an addict's mouth.

I would like to thank Chris Tillman for encouraging me to turn my cathartic writings into a book to share my story with others. I would like to thank my mother for being the best mother she could be despite astronomical obstacles that faced a single parent in the sixties with no financial support from her first husband and an abusive second husband. Mom, we never knew how hard life was for you because you made sure we came first and you protected us the best you could! To my son Bryce, I would like to thank you for all of your accomplishments and helping me as a father not have a complete melt down because at least I knew I wasn't a complete failure as a Dad. You gave me the hope and courage to continue to try to understand your brother and his drug addiction and eventually the addiction of others. And a special Thank You to my editor, Robin Martin of Two Songbirds Press, for believing in my story and my ability to convey it. I couldn't have completed this without you!

Part I: Defining Moments
Chapter 1: The Medicine Cabinet

I sit alone in my new quad truck with its twenty-two inch rims; it looks like some twenty year-old spoiled brat has decked it out. I am tucked away in a remote parking space at a retail shopping center. No one would normally park this far from the grocery store, which anchors an array of businesses, at least not this late at night in this sparsely populated lot. I know this place well, as this is where my wife and I buy our groceries. It is in an upper class neighborhood serving the wealthy residents who live in their posh homes nearby. The front of my truck faces a short decorative fence, which borders a greenbelt area, and I stare across the wetlands that the railing protects. As I sit, I think about the circumstances in my life that brought me to this spot. I am alert to my surroundings but distracted by my thoughts. The fingers on my left hand slowly stroke my bottom lip and then downward across my graying goatee. It is eerily quiet, but my mind pounds with the noise in my head. My attention should be entirely on the task at hand and not the events in my life that led me here, but my mind hiccoughs.

I am here because this is where the drug dealers will meet me. They have $2500 in cash in exchange for the one hundred 80 milligram Oxycontin tablets which are in a small plastic bottle, tucked away into my jacket pocket. I have just turned fifty years old, which is older than the combined age of the young couple who will be meeting me. It is early 2009, and the drug I have in my pocket was not even available when I was a teenager. In my younger days the contents in my pocket would have been cocaine or marijuana, but times have changed.

The eventual recipients of these pills will be the addicts who crave them more than a next meal or the love of their family, or anything for that matter. The pills are small, round and an odd green color—a powerful prescription drug manufactured to relieve severe pain. They are essentially synthetic heroin, and much sought after by the drug addicts who litter your streets, work alongside you and perhaps sit next to you at a family dinner. They are daughters or sons or parents. The street price for these pills could reach up to $80 each, while the co-pay at the pharmacy for the insured who are prescribed these pills could be as little as $10 for a quantity of ninety. That is quite a tidy profit for all involved, and the sellers do not care what casualties wait. That is about all that stays the same in the drug world decade after decade.

The pill commonly referred to by the street name "Oxy" does not get swallowed by addicts in the way the pharmaceutical companies intended. To intensify the effect of the drug, they consume the pills in alternative ways: First, they remove the time-release coating that covers the pill, by either scraping it off with their fingernail or using a wet paper towel. Then, they crush the tablet into a powder and snort it. When snorting the Oxy begins to clog up and destroy their noses, or just isn't getting them high enough, the addict places the pill whole, without the coating, onto a small square of aluminum foil, and holds a lighter underneath. The addict rolls the pill around the foil in an odd balancing act, so as not to lose the pill off the edge of the hot foil, or to leave it in one hot spot too long. As it slides from side to side the lighter is moved just ahead of it. The pill slowly vaporizes as it is cooked from beneath. A thin line of fumes from the pill is released into the air, and the addict inhales the vapor through a stem pipe. Addicts hardly notice that their fingers and thumbs burn; blisters form where the flame licks back from the bottom of the foil. As the pill slides back and forth, it leaves behind a zigzagging black mark resembling a line made by an indelible pen. This technique is called "chasing the dragon," and is reminiscent of a technique for ingesting heroin, Oxy's unfashionable, yet omnipresent, cousin.

When addicts become so addicted that they cannot afford the quantity of Oxy they need to satisfy their cravings, as the appetite exceeds the budget, it is time for the next phase of this vicious cycle. Addicts will do what they said they would never do. Steal money. Sell their bodies to strangers. Encourage their girlfriend or wife to sell her body. Anything to get the cash they desperately need to feed the demon that owns them. The most extreme way to increase Oxy's effect is to reduce the powder to a liquid, draw it into a syringe, and shoot it into their veins, warming them from the inside out. Sound familiar? There is nothing more glamorous about this drug than heroin. The same addiction, the same diseases, the same low-down disgusting lying homeless in the alley and piss your pants drug—Oxy is essentially synthetic heroin. And the last step, when addicts can no longer afford Oxy, is to get on heroin.

Lives are ruined or lost completely to Oxycontin, which, unlike the drugs of the past, is found in the medicine cabinets of parents, grandparents and patients with severe pain all over this world. Some of these patients lose their prescription unsuspectingly to family members or caregivers who steal it for the street value. Other patients have discovered the street value so they beg their medical providers for more, claiming their pain has escalated and they need it more frequently to stop their suffering—then, they sell it.

The young couple coming to buy my Oxy know me as the latter— an old guy with a script. I know they are both addicts and I know the boyfriend, Steve, is a big time Oxy dealer, selling it faster than he can get it. I also know that his girlfriend, Ashley, sells her young body—he demands it—to pull her own weight in this sick relationship anchored in addiction.

I know this because I've hired her.

I look straight ahead at the entryway to this shopping center which is a narrow bridge spanning over the wetland preserve. A light fog hovers above the shallow water and dissipates into the cattails that line its shore. It is getting darker by the moment, but my eyes have adjusted and I can clearly see the cars that cross. I eliminate them as they drive past. I am looking for one of two cars I believe they will be driving. Will it be the red Dodge Charger or the white Lexus sedan or perhaps a complete surprise? One way or the next, they know where I am and what I am driving and exactly where I am parked. I have met Ashley, so she should have no problem identifying me. I focus on the occupants of car after car. I am far too tense to be sleepy, but I am dazed by the constant parade of memories and possibilities that march through my head as I attempt to digest thousands of thoughts, hell bent on answering the question: Why do I sit here?

It has been many years since I have been involved in a drug deal, and my assumption is that the process hasn't changed much. My mother has been through too much pain and I can't

Defining Moments

imagine what affect it would have on her to visit another family member in jail if things go badly tonight. I think about the deep secret I have now and what my mother would think, and those defining moments that led me here.

Chapter 2: Small Town Whispers

Sometimes life's secrets begin with life itself. My mother discovered she was pregnant with my older brother Thomas while she was still a high school student in a tiny town in Kansas. To this day the town still has brick streets and tiny homes that are a throwback to simpler times. The town is so small that the phonebook is about the size of a comic book. It was 1957 and she was impregnated by her boyfriend in the back seat of his parents' car. My mother and father decided to sneak out to a neighboring town and get married after they discovered her pregnancy. After their wedding, they returned to their respective homes each night, keeping their secret. They did not know how or when they would break the news to their families. But they had overlooked a tell-tale sign of their nuptials: The event would be published under "wedding announcements" in that little town's newspaper, just a few miles down a rural road.

Their secret was revealed over the high school intercom when they were both summoned from their classes to the Principal's office. The announcer, heard by all who attended this rural school in the center of Hoisington, Kansas, called my father's name, Richard T. DeHaven, and then my mother's newly acquired married name, Karla June DeHaven. It echoed through the classrooms, with a collective gasp from students and teachers. They were excused from class, walked through the desks that lined the classroom, all eyes following them out the door. Their parents stood with the principal ready for their arrival at the office. As they entered the room it wasn't hard to see the anger and disappointment. They were from different sides of this small town. My father's dad was a butcher, his wife a seamstress. My mother's dad was an oil rig grunt of American-Indian decent, and his wife, a meek submissive homemaker. Neither parent thought the other was good enough for their child, let alone the fact that they were both still children.

Defining Moments

Once the reason for the marriage was revealed, their parents accepted it as best as they could. My father's parents arranged for them to live together in a small home while they finished school and awaited the birth of their baby. It was the late fifties and a pregnant teenager was an embarrassment. Shame followed the couple wherever they went.

Thomas Richard was born on a cold December day to parents who were children themselves. I followed just thirteen months later, and another brother was born fourteen months later and died almost immediately after his birth. My mother at twenty years old had two toddlers and had to accept the death of her third baby. Years later, I returned to this town and located the home we first shared. The home, which had since been converted into a one car garage, still had the old front door located next to a single car garage door that had been put in place of what was once the front window. It seemed impossible that it could have ever have been anything but a garage.

Chapter 3: The Set Up

The lights of another car coming over the bridge do not belong to either vehicle I am expecting, so I examine the occupants. It is a man and his wife about my age, so I look away quickly as to not draw attention to myself. I know I've got to wait patiently, as this drug deal is important to me and my family. I need it to happen. Another thing hasn't changed about drug deals in all the years since my last: Buyers are always late to arrive and usually short on cash with lame excuses throughout the process. I am expecting $2500 in cash as agreed and I hope that the deal goes smoothly so I can go home safely to my wife and sons.

I don't want any problems, and I don't want to see any weapons. Drug dealing has never been an honorable profession, so anything could happen. Though I have never met the buyer, I have been assured by his girlfriend that he will have the money and the deal will take only a few minutes. I also know that Ashley is seriously addicted to Oxy. After we first met—at her apartment—she called me several times just to get a few pills to hold her over until we could meet for this drug deal. I have refused her every time as I have told her that we will meet just the one time and exchange all the drugs for the money at once. She has tried to entice me with her young body in exchange for a couple Oxy, but I have resisted the temptation.

The first time Ashley and I met, I had the pleasure of seeing her naked body, but my goal is not to see it again. My goal is to do this drug deal. Her actions highlight that she is seriously addicted and that is not comforting when I am taking her word that Steve is a trustworthy drug dealer, as if there is such a thing. Another car approaches and it is white, but I cannot tell the make of the vehicle. As it passes, I check it out and see that it is a woman with two small children. She is handing a baby bottle towards a car seat in the back. A young boy sitting in the front passenger seat stares back at me as if to say, "What are you looking at?" I was once that baby in the backseat and my brother that inquisitive one in the front. My father wouldn't have been in the car either. He disappeared long before I could commit him to my young memory.

Defining Moments

Chapter 4: The Sixties and the Single Mom

I don't remember many details of my early childhood. As much as I try, I cannot visualize my father, Richard, in any setting. I remember my mother, my brother, grandparents, babysitters, uncles, friends, and different events, but I just can't place my father anywhere. My parents divorced in the early sixties and my brother Thomas and I were very young. We took a train ride from Kansas to California; my mother told us we were on an adventure. We were far too young to comprehend divorce so there was no reason for her to explain. Our dogs, Ringo and Trixie, were caged in the back of the train, surrounded by luggage. To get to them, it required passing through a designated men's area—occupied by men only. My mother could not accompany us. Smoke filled the air and men of all different types stared at Thomas and me as we huddled together passing through their compartment. Our mother told us not to speak or look at them and we obeyed as best we could. The ride was long, and I am certain that we were a handful on a train for days on end.

We moved into a three-bedroom home with my grandparents in Los Angeles, California. My Uncle Dan lived there also. My grandfather was a very volatile person, a hateful man, and he clashed with his son—my Uncle Dan—often. They physically fought, and my uncle was no match for his father. My grandfather, a retired oil driller from Oklahoma and Kansas, drank a lot. His skin was Indian-dark, and the wrinkles on his face were deep. My brother and I would hide when they fought, and my mother would hold us if she was there, placing her hands over our ears and cradling us close to her. Her body muffled the sounds. She would rock slightly while humming or singing quietly so we would drift off to anyplace but there.

We stayed because we had no place else to go, just as my uncle and my grandmother did.

My grandmother was a stark contrast to my grandfather. She always had a bright smile and she treated us with an abundance of love. She was a heavy woman and her girth made her seem even shorter than she was. She had an infectious laugh. Grandma worked at a department store named Zodies. On occasion, my mother would take us to the store to visit her on her break. We would run from aisle to aisle searching for her brightly colored smock. One of the few times I ever remember eating out was when we shared her lunch break and ate hot dogs and popcorn at the department store cafeteria. I still think of Grandma whenever I walk into a discount store and smell the snack bar. We lived with our grandparents longer than we should have, but my mother had little choice.

My mother, still young and very attractive, was saddled with the responsibility of two young boys who knew nothing about her predicament. She made sure we never felt like we were a burden, but as I look back I know it must have been so difficult for her. She never complained and we always felt her love. She worked as a carhop at a Bob's Big Boy hamburger joint and she wore roller skates to serve the drive up customers in their cars. My Uncle Dan would take us there at night to visit her and she could sometimes sneak us some food. We would watch her roller-skating from car to car and back inside to retrieve her food orders. Uncle Dan was a hero to us as he was the only consistent male figure in our life. The drive up stations at Bob's Big Boy were filled with a variety of Hot Rods and they were in all shapes, colors and sizes. The engines revved and the tires squealed consistently as the parade of cars cruised through. It was an exciting place and a formative moment for both Thomas and me, and helped to cement our lifelong love of muscle cars. We were so proud of our mother and we loved to tell our friends where she worked. Our friends would openly wonder why a mother would be working at all.

It was very unusual in that time period not to have a father. Our friends were puzzled by our missing parent, our working mother, and our home with our grandparents. We were an oddity in the sixties to almost everyone we met. Other parents would question us when we visited our friend's homes, extracting information that we were ignorant enough to share and which likely hit the gossip circuit immediately. The other mothers were threatened by our mother, as she was beautiful and divorced! I would later realize how poorly my mother was treated by other mothers, and how she endured many unwanted sexual advances and groping by their spouses and her employers. It was the sixties, and my mother was damaged goods in their eyes; she was vulnerable.

We eventually moved out of my grandparents' home to an apartment in Los Angeles and then to a small rental house in Burbank that backed up to a military plant. Barrels of who-knows-what lined the side of our back fence. I guess the rent is cheaper when you live next to a toxic dump! We had a yard for our dogs and new friends to meet, and we settled into this little house. My brother and I still shared a room, as we always had, and we still had each other, despite another change in schools and friends.

At dinner sometimes, Mom wouldn't eat. She would say she wasn't hungry or offer some excuse. I would later realize that she fed us first because she was so broke she couldn't afford to feed herself. In all the years after the divorce, she had never received a dime in child support from my biological father, Richard. There were times at this house when my mother would have us hide in the closet with her. This would happen when the rent was past due. She would make a game out of it, but you could see the fear in her eyes, as this was no game. The landlord would come to our house to collect the rent personally. He would first knock on the door and then let himself in the house. We were quiet in the closet in my mother's room. The landlord would walk through the house yelling my mother's first name, "Karla . . . Karla . . . Karla!" We could hear him approaching the bedroom as the volume of his voice increased. We watched through the slats in the closet door as he would open her dresser drawers and rummage through her belongings, including her undergarments, while looking around over his shoulder, still yelling her name. Eventually he would leave and somehow mom would come up with the rent to keep a roof over our heads for another month.

We were getting old enough to know that we were different than most families in many ways, but we always knew we had a loving mother. Thomas and I also knew that the only other consistent thing in our life was each other. We were very close in size and we were often mistaken as twins, although I had blond hair and he had brown. We fought like all brothers did, but we had always shared a bedroom and we talked each other to sleep every night.

Defining Moments

I never remember my mother dating much, so I think she was careful not to introduce us to any suitor until it was more serious. She eventually met a man who she was serious about, Dino. He would sometimes bring food we were not accustomed to eating, like steak. I had no memory of any man ever giving us a gift or anything of the sort before, but occasionally he would bring us a trinket to our mother's delight. He was a big man with a dark complexion and jet-black hair and he would often talk on the phone in his native Greek. Thomas and I had never heard someone speak in a foreign language so it was intriguing.

My mom soon married Dino and we officially had a stepfather. Shortly after they were married we moved north to Sacramento. It was a six-hour drive from where my grandparents and uncle lived. We said our goodbyes to our sobbing grandmother and to all our friends and entered a new chapter in our lives. I was in the fifth grade. Thomas was in sixth.

Chapter 5: Connections

My disposable cell phone rings and it is Ashley. She tries to get me to change my location and meet her at her apartment across town.

"I am waiting where I fucking told you I would wait. I am not moving anywhere," I hissed into the crack-berry—my nickname for the phone.

The thought of walking into some apartment and getting clunked over the head for drugs is not an option. This is the second time Steve and Ashley are supposed to meet me for this buy, and the last time they decided not to show after I wasted hours listening to their phone calls buying more time or trying to get me to drive somewhere else.

"I have no intention of moving anywhere, so get your shit together or this deal is off." I tell her this is her last chance to get the Oxy and I will be waiting in the spot I told her. "Hurry up, or I will sell the drugs to someone else, just like I did the last time you flaked!" I push the end call button on this cheap pre-paid cell phone that I purchased just to do this deal and I toss it onto the console of the truck. I didn't want these drug dealers to know my real name or have my actual cell phone number. Steve and Ashley know my elder son, Brandon, and my second son, Bryce, but they do not know I am their father or that there is any connection between us. They know me under my chosen alias, "Bill" and when I am done with this deal I will toss this pre-paid phone which I have nicknamed the crack-berry in the nearest dumpster and never be in this situation again. I am tired of sitting in this parking lot staring out over the tall weeds and watching every car and truck that drives in. The lot becomes more deserted as the night slowly drags on and the skies darken.

Defining Moments

Chapter 6: Change Doesn't Ask Permission

When my brother, mom and I moved from Kansas to Los Angeles, we lost touch with our grandparents and uncles on my father's side. When we moved to Sacramento we lost touch with our grandparents and uncle who we had come to know as our family from my mom's side. Now that we were in Sacramento, we quickly discovered that we had new grandparents, aunts, uncles and many cousins in this large Greek family. New traditions, strange food, and apparently, we were now a new religion—it was Greek to me.

It is odd as a ten year old to have someone introduced to you as your new family. "This is your aunt, this is your uncle, and this is your cousin" . . . They didn't look like us and they didn't act like us. They spoke Greek amongst themselves making Thomas and me feel like outsiders, imagining that they were judging us, something we had become accustomed to. Large get-togethers were common and we were often at some family event. The Greeks do love to host ambitious parties. Every birthday and holiday was a huge gathering with all sorts of foods we had never seen and as much as we tried, we couldn't pronounce. Entire lambs roasted slowly over open pit fires. Hamburger rolled inside grape leaves. Lasagna in white sauce instead of red. We were not just in a new town, but in a whole new world.

Thomas and I stuck together, were confidants and support for one another. We were getting older and wiser so we were more aware of what was going on around us. Our stepfather Dino turned out to be a mystery man with a past that didn't add up and a temper that escalated with every drink he poured down his throat. He had a painted on smile that couldn't be trusted. It was the same smile every time and it was anything but genuine and it could turn to angry gritted teeth in a moment. He was terrifyingly loud and strong, and we were not accustomed to being told what to do by a man. We did our best to stay out of his way, particularly when he was drinking, but he would always find us.

My brother Thomas and I had become very good at yard work and chores as we learned to perform them with perfection or pay the price of Dino's disappointment. Every weekend was filled with hour upon hour of yard work at Dino's command. If we ran out of work to do, Dino would have us move a scrap woodpile from one end of the backyard to another, then back again if he wasn't done with us. Sometimes Dino would stand in the backyard and direct us with a garden hose nozzle, spraying us from one chore to the next. Dino was sick. We never knew when we were going to get knocked across the room. We were often treated like unwanted animals. We wondered why this was happening to us but at the same time we wondered if the same thing was happening in the families across the street.

Our half-brother, Harry (named after Dino's father) was soon born. Then, my stepfather had even less regard for us. We were second-class citizens to his "real" son. My mother was also abused. She stayed, as so many abused women do, because her only options would lead us back to poverty and uncertainty, and also because Dino threatened to take my little brother to Greece where she would never see him again. She protected us and herself as best as she could and she likely hoped for better days. Back then we didn't have options as kids either. There were no toll free hotline numbers to call to safely report abuse and we knew better than to tell anyone what was happening behind closed doors. If we kept our mouths shut we would hopefully avoid making him even angrier.

He weighed over 200 pounds and he could do some damage any way he beat us. The primary goal when getting beaten by a person nearly twice one's size is to limit injuries and not escalate the violence because there is no winning. I had seen this tactic with my grandfather and my uncle, and my brother and I were now in a similar situation. When someone saw the marks or bruises on our bodies we lied so we didn't get a repeat performance. Gym teachers or other kids during showers after PE class asked the most questions. We just blamed it on each other as a fight between brothers. We just learned to live with it and survive. We became quite the fighters at school and other kids learned not to screw with us or we would beat them down. It was just something one gets good at when one is in constant training.

My parents —I had been instructed to refer to Dino as my father—entertained a lot. The rooms would fill with drinkers and drunks, for it was the seventies and the cocktails were flowing freely. The money was coming in heavy and Mom and Dino lived a lavish lifestyle. They went out to dinner at fancy restaurants often and everyone knew their names as they entered. He had his own table at several places and the same personal waiter; he was treated like royalty. I remember he would carry a rare $1000 bill and attempt to pay his bill with it to shock the waiters who would say, "We can't change that!" My mom was wearing fur coats and new jewelry all the time. Dino was "in the import-export" business. We would later find out that he was involved in a criminal enterprise, and during this time was smuggling diamonds.

It was not unusual for Dino's associates to come to the house with weapons inside their jackets. When they played poker, stacks of hundred dollar bills spilled across the table, and one of the requirements to sit at the table was to put your gun in a pile of weapons across the room. I guess they didn't want the loser to play his trump card with a pistol! My brother and I hustled drinks for them for small tips. After we were told to go to bed, we would hide behind the counter that blocked the table where they played cards. We could stay there late into the night and hear details of these shady lives. They all had odd nicknames. One man was called "The Painter" and I have no idea where the name came from but I did know that if they needed someone's house "painted" that this man was going there to kill them. He was a hit man, plain and simple! Their conversations were graphic. One night my stepfather won a big poker hand that included a man's car, a classic Bentley! This man was called the "Undertaker" but I am not sure what he did. Maybe he really was an undertaker but I doubt it. Another man they called "The Banker," and he really was a banker but he was crooked as a stick. They had something on him because he would do whatever my stepfather told him to do. I remember going to the bank and walking in or out with bags of cash. The "Judge" was actually a Judge and he lived next door. He was a nice man. I babysat his kids and watched his house while he vacationed, and did some odd jobs for him. My stepfather and his associates spoke openly about their various girlfriends and the dual lives they led. Dino also had a girlfriend and a separate apartment in which he put her up. My brother and I were young and we were afraid of this man so we didn't disclose what we knew to anyone.

Defining Moments

When I was about fourteen years old, I missed curfew, which I knew was a big mistake. I tried to open the door with no sound. As I turned in the entryway to close the door as quietly as I had opened it, I felt a presence. I turned around and two hands were on my neck choking me and shoving me against the door. Dino, in the darkness, had a grip on my neck that he would not release. I grabbed his wrist and tried to push his hands off to no avail. I couldn't breathe, so I couldn't talk. It was oddly silent except for a pinging sound, as if someone was dropping pennies in a pan. It was the sound of the puka shells from the necklace I was wearing landing on the tile floor beneath me. Ping, ping, puh dit dit, ping. More of the shells fell and bounced along the tile. I could not get a next breath. I tried to pry his fingers from my neck but I couldn't get my fingers between his to loosen his grip. I finally got one of my hands wrapped around one of his fingers, but it wasn't enough to free myself. I believed it was going to be over soon and I was going to die. I could see him clearly now that my eyes had adjusted to the darkness, and he looked like a madman just inches from my face as he continued to push me up against the door. He didn't mutter a word from his gritted teeth. I don't even know if my feet were on the ground. I must have passed out because I don't remember what happened next. I awoke in the entryway and he was gone. I rolled to my knees and I could hear the crackle of the puka shells beneath the weight of my body. I felt the shells of my coveted necklace sticking to my palms as I tried to steady myself on all fours. With my focus and clarity returning, I quietly gathered up all the shells I could, put them in my pockets and went to my room. I was alive, but the puka shell necklace was a goner.

On one final occasion, my parents were having a large party at the house. I was sitting at a desk in my room doing some schoolwork and I could hear the guests' loud voices in the hallway beyond my door. Suddenly my door burst open and slammed against the wall. It was Dino, and he commanded me to stand up. I could see some party guests in the hallway behind him. The sound of the door and his voice had them looking at me from around his large frame. Their conversations stopped as their attention was drawn to the commotion. I stood and Dino directed me to approach him. He was obviously drunk and I could see the usual crazed look in his eyes. He started rambling something about how I didn't like him or respect him and I quickly claimed I did. I was a lanky fifteen year old, probably about 5'8", 140 pounds. He stepped towards me as I obeyed his wish for me to come to him. He hit me so fast I didn't see it coming and I flew backwards onto the desktop. All four legs of the desk broke beneath the impact of my body. I lay there stunned on my back. As Dino walked towards me, I could see the crowd of guests rushing in behind him. He straddled me and I gathered my legs towards my chest with my arms crossed in front of my face to protect myself. He looked like a killer standing over me, his eyes big, his teeth gritted and his right fist well above his head poised to pound me again. I straightened my right leg out as a kick upward directly into his crotch as hard and fast as I could. His body folded around my foot. He fell backwards on the ground exposing the crowd of onlookers who stood behind him. I stood up and walked by him, looking down at him curled and rolling in obvious agony. I walked through the crowd, which parted as I approached. Another defining moment. I went to stay with a friend, and I never went home again as long as Dino was alive.

I promised myself over and over again that if I ever had children, I would never beat them.

Defining Moments

Chapter 7: Now the Truth Comes Out

My phone is ringing, but this time it is the hands free unit in my ear, my real cell phone number, not the crack-berry. I am not here alone. In fact, there are about twenty undercover officers with me, but I'm no cop. On the phone is lead undercover narcotics officer Denny White. Officer White wants to do a last minute sound check on the wire that I am wearing taped to my back. It seems that my lack of noise has caused the undercover officers who surround me in cars, vans and bushes to become concerned that they have lost sound. They haven't heard a word from me since my last crack-berry conversation with Ashley, the suspect that I have set up in exchange for dropping pending drug dealing charges.

They are not my charges. They belong to my son. He is the real drug dealer. I'm just trying to be a good dad.

My last conversation with Ashley seemed a little muffled and the cops want to make sure they get a clear recording of the drug deal. The reason I am here and have insisted that I do this is complicated. I think I am here to save my family the anguish of watching another family member go to jail, not wanting to relive the time I watched my brother Thomas go to a federal prison for dealing drugs many years before. Maybe I am here because I just don't know how to be a father and despite my attempt to be the best father I never had, I have failed miserably!

Officer White coaches me through the sound check. Apparently the microphone at my jacket collar is slipping down and everything is muffled. I am told to pull it up, but warned that it might easily disconnect and if it did, the bust would be aborted. After some light tugging on the mic to get it between my collar and my neck, Officer White says the sound is good. As we talk on the phone, he assures me that I am doing fine and I should continue to hold my position no matter how hard Ashley and Steve try to get me to go to their location. The attempt to move me is a tactic the narcotics officers know well. The goal of the drug dealer will be to get me on his ground and on his terms. With so

Defining Moments

many officers surrounding me in a variety of cars, trucks, vans and on foot around the parking lot, acting like patrons of the nearby stores, there is no way they could all uproot and follow me to some new location. Not to mention that marked police cars are waiting within striking distance of the retail center.

I know the cops can hear everything I say so I spare them my nervous singing and limit my comments, fighting my compulsion to curse wickedly at them. I'm staring off across the wetlands, connecting with known drug dealers, talking to undercover narcotics officers on my personal cell phone, feeling a wire taped to my body and extending up to my neck, holding a bottle filled with one hundred Oxys in my jacket pocket. What brought me here? Where did things get so completely fucked up?

Chapter 8: Boy Meets World

I officially moved out of my parents' home when I was fifteen years old, thirty-five years ago. I didn't have a driver's license yet, but I had a learner's permit. I had no car and I walked, bummed a ride or hitchhiked if I needed to get someplace like work or high school. It was not easy living on my own and finding roommates at such a young age, but I managed. After a short stint of crashing on couches or extra bedrooms of several friends, I rented a room at a house with some other kids near my age.

I was still in high school and I wanted to graduate, but I also needed money to live on. Rent, food, utilities and various expenses were all new to me. The father of my girlfriend Lori was an executive of a supermarket chain, and he made some calls and got me an interview. The manager explained to me that he would love to hire me but he had a hiring freeze on everyone but minorities. I had no idea what this meant so I asked, and he explained to me all the types of minorities that he could hire, including, American Indian. I said, "Hey, my grandfather was half American Indian," and he hired me on the spot. I have never used my heritage in any way since that day. It felt wrong to me that because of my ancestry I could be hired, but I needed a job and this one paid well. I worked the 3 p.m. to midnight shift bagging groceries and stocking shelves. The money was good and it helped me provide for myself.

I purchased a 1967 Chevelle SS for $1,000 and I spent a lot of time and money trying to make it faster than the next. Hot Rods were as popular in the seventies as I remembered them in the days of Bob's Big Boy Drive Ins. I adored working on this Chevelle and meeting others who enjoyed the same passion. Even though I lived on my own, I was still a kid and I knew no better than to live like one. I found myself associated with a group at school referred to by some as "hot-rodders" and by others as "burnouts." The hot-rodders loved and raced every kind of

Defining Moments

American muscle car you could imagine, and this was what drew me to them.

As every school has its "jocks," "nerds," "burnouts," and other cliques and the reps that go along with them, it is difficult for an impressionable adolescent to avoid. The hot-rodders had a "bad boy" reputation affiliated with drug use. Many hot-rodders did drugs and many of us sold drugs (usually to the jocks). It was the days of cocaine and pot, and I saw and consumed my share of it. Thomas became one of the bigger drug dealers in town. His house was filled with booze and drugs of all types. Cocaine was the most popular, that, and pot; but magic mushrooms and acid were also available. It was the late seventies, after all.

We were also surrounded by some pretty tough guys and nobody really messed with us. After years of sparring with a two hundred pound Greek, I was pretty tough myself. We would host evening boxing matches in the living room of the house I rented with my friends. We had no furniture in that room. A boxing match would start with one person calling out another person to fight. You could decline, but you would endure the collective shaming of the crowd. Several sets of boxing gloves were available and once both fighters had their gloves on, the games would begin. Cowering in a corner was never a good strategy as the crowd only pushed you back to the center. The room erupted when the action was good and the fights were a scrappy version of actual boxing. The fight was over when you surrendered or you were knocked out.

I fought many times and I do not remember ever losing. As I said, I had grown up facing a much tougher opponent than anyone in the room. I was rarely injured because I had learned to protect myself from the powerful blows of my stepfather and I knew how to look for an opening and drop my opponent. By this time I was close to six feet tall and about 175 pounds. I was in great shape and I had endured physical punishment as training.

Drag racing wasn't easy on a car, and since we were constantly racing, constantly striving to make the Chevelle faster, inevitably something was always broken. Hitchhiking to and from work became a regular event, and I often got rides from the same people every afternoon. Frequently I ended up walking home at midnight. When I did get home there was usually a gathering of my roommates and their friends. Pot smoke always filled the air.

The family room had an array of donated couches, chairs, and beanbags gathered by the roommates and friends. A long curled phone cord hung from the center of the ceiling with a roach clip taped to it. This was a convenient way to pass a joint around the room without ever leaving your chair. The clip swung from smoker to smoker. Every day, I got up and went to school early and my daily routine would repeat itself.

Somehow I willed myself to stick it out at school despite my surroundings and the influences of my peers. I don't know what it was that enabled me to do this, to not fall entirely into the wasteland of addiction and entitlement. Biology? Character? It's inexplicable, really. All of my roommates had dropped out of high school, but somehow I continued; although my grades sucked, they were passing grades. In my senior year I only took classes until noon because that was all I needed to graduate. I got another job at a local restaurant for the lunch shift as well as any days I was off from the grocery store. I realized at an early age that nobody was going to give me anything and if I wanted something I would need to earn it. If I didn't succeed, I wouldn't survive!

Somewhere around this time, I decided to try and find my biological father, Richard, a natural thing for a young man my age to want to do, right? So I tracked him down and called him. Richard was living in Arkansas and had been for many years. We talked on the phone and upon discovering he would be near Thomas and me on a business trip, arranged a meeting at a hotel. Thomas begged out at the last minute, and without contacting Richard I brought my friend Bill with me for the drive into the bay area. When I knocked on the door of the hotel room, my father opened the door looked at me, called me Thomas, and then he looked at Bill and called him by my name. He didn't even know what his own kids looked like. We spent a brief time in the hotel room getting our names and heritage correct, then were off to dinner. During the dinner, Richard asked if I could "score some toot" which I discovered meant find cocaine. Well, I didn't need to look much past my pocket to score, so we ended up getting drunk and snorting toot to commemorate our father and son reunion. At the time, it seemed like, "Wow, my dad is cool," but I later realized how sick it all truly was.

Defining Moments

The fact is, this man was never a father or a dad or anything to me. Richard basically knocked my mother up in high school, married her, had another son and abandoned her and his sons while they were still babies. He never paid my mother a dime in child support. My mother tried to warn me when I decided I wanted to meet him, but as only time would tell, trying to tell your teenage son anything is a virtual impossibility.

After I graduated high school, I went to Hawaii with a friend to live. The simple reason? I was eighteen and that was drinking age in Hawaii. I quit my grocery job and took the money I had saved and headed off to the islands. Once there, we pretty much surfed, drank and looked for pot. We were on an extended vacation and my best friend Pete, who went with me, was a spoiled brat with an endless supply of money from his father who was one of the Greek associates of my stepfather, Dino. We were bound to get in trouble or find ourselves in danger and that is exactly what happened.

One day a very tall guy walking the streets just outside our apartment in Waikiki approached us. He told us he had the best quality pot at his apartment. Once inside his apartment, he went into a back room to get the pot. As we waited in the kitchen, a group of large men walked in with knives, mugged us then threw us out. The oldest trick in the effing book. It was quick and easy for them and we got to leave without a knife in our gut. Who were we going to tell? About a month after this robbery, I looked out the window of our apartment and to my surprise saw the guy who had set us up for the robbery! He was a tall lanky guy with a bushel of hair so he was easy to spot. I dragged Pete to the window to show him the guy. We hustled down the stairs and I walked straight towards this guy and he didn't recognize me at all. He asked me if I wanted to buy some pot in exactly the same way he did before. I said, "Sure, should we follow you to the same apartment so your friends can rob us again?" He looked shocked and before he could say a word, I dropped him with one punch where he stood and it didn't stop there. This guy was begging for his life as I pummeled him and Pete just watched in shock. I made this scumbag give me every penny he had on him and we never saw him again.

Another day, as we walked away from a beach after swimming, a police car pulled over and started to question us.

They were big Hawaiian guys with badges and they did not like howlies. They grabbed us, roughed us up and handcuffed us because we were two high white guys. They drove us deep into a sugar cane plantation. We were not going to the police station. Pete and I sat in the back of this police car on our bound hands in silence. They eventually pulled us out of the car and beat the shit out of us. They undid our handcuffs when they were done, emptied our pockets of every dollar, and even took the pot we had. They left us in the field and all we knew to do was to walk back the way we came. We hitchhiked to the airport and stood outside where the planes were de-boarding. We hustled an unsuspecting tourist into buying our surfboards so we could return to California. I collect-called my mother from Waikiki once we knew what flight we would be on and she was surprised to hear my voice since we hadn't talked in months. She picked us up at the airport and I think her head almost turned in a circle when she saw us. Our hair was down to the middle of our backs and we were as dark as natives.

It was crazy times then.

Defining Moments

Chapter 9: Times They Are a Changing

Back in Sacramento, freebasing and disco were big. Before long, one of my roommates was busted with an abundance of cocaine and I narrowly missed the arrest. I was literally driving away from the house and saw cop cars coming down the street toward it. I watched in the rearview mirror as they surrounded the house and I knew he was inside, high on free-base and well supplied with cocaine. Shortly thereafter I decided to move away and find a new environment. Sacramento seemed like it was now completely out of control! People were staying up for days on end freebasing, and it was not fun being around someone focused on his next fix or dolling out drugs to fellow addicts.

I moved to Lake Tahoe because they still didn't give a shit how anyone dressed and that was fine with me. No white polyester pants here! My best friend Pete and I opened a waterbed and hot tub store in North Lake Tahoe called Sierra Waterbeds and Hot Tubs—a venture his father funded. I was selling waterbeds and this new invention called a portable hot tub. Pete and I still drank and partied and the drugs were still around. Unlike most of the people I knew, I managed to be truly a recreational user with no tendencies towards addiction. But I am no prude, and we had our share of parties and events in Tahoe and at the waterbed store. When you put a bunch of twenty year olds and their friends in a retail store that has working hot tubs and waterbeds, things can quickly spiral out of control. We had no window coverings and our parties were in plain view of anyone who put their nose against the windows. It was a voyeurs' paradise and I am sure we entertained a lot of shocked window shoppers late into the night!

Pete proved to be a bad choice of a business partner, as his use of cocaine escalated to the point of total addiction. In less than a year he would snort everything he could get his hands on. He was stealing money from the checking account and drop-shipping inventory from our business directly to drug dealers to feed his habit. My own brother Thomas was one of the many drug dealers receiving this merchandise for pennies on the dollar in exchange for cocaine and marijuana. This would be one of the many actions that would drive a wedge between Thomas and me as drugs and money started to always come before family. It hurt me deeply to contemplate Thomas's complete disregard for our relationship as brothers and his choice to take this merchandise from my addicted partner while knowing full well that it would financially destroy my business and thus me.

Pete had already disappeared for several weeks when I discovered what he was doing, but it was too late and the business closed within a month after the invoices for all of these portable spas and waterbeds started arriving. The checking account had been completely drained of any operating capital. Bad business partner, and bad best friend. My girlfriend at the time, Karen, had hidden her drug habit from me, and by the time I discovered it, she had emptied our joint savings account and was screwing my ex-partner/best friend, Pete. They were both very addicted to cocaine and I guess they belonged together because neither one of them belonged with me. I went to her apartment where I caught them together. I beat him within an inch of his life in front of her. Karen and her roommate did everything they could to pull me off of him, but my rage for his complete abandonment of our friendship in so many ways had escalated to the perfect storm. It seemed he had taken everything from me and he had been my closest friend for the last six years and I snapped.

This was a defining moment in my life, where I began to truly understand what drugs could make you do. Pete and Karen later married, had a couple of kids and, in his late twenties, Pete died of a heroin overdose.

I moved to the south side of the lake and began selling radio advertising. I still called Thomas in Sacramento often, as family is family, and he was about all I had left in that category and he was all I had growing up. He was my big brother and there was no changing that. I tried to forgive him for the part he played in my business failure, but I never confronted him; I just buried my resentment. When I did visit his home it was hard for him to hide the bounty of furnishings that adorned his drug kingpin house. Many of his belongings had obviously come from my defunct store.

Thomas was dealing drugs on a very large scale and was about to be busted. There were a couple of occasions when I was at his home in Sacramento when the cocaine was piled so high on his glass top dining table that you needed to be careful that it did not slide off on the floor. Scales were pushed tightly up to the edge of the mound of white rocky powder as if to build a barrier around it. Sometimes several people would be working in sync, doing everything from cutting the cocaine to increase profits, to weighing it and bagging it for sale. The cocaine was put in small baggies or tiny glass vials in as little as one gram or scooped into zip lock bags weighing up to one pound. The constant consumption of the cocaine by the helpers appeared to be the payment for the effort of assisting in the process. People would come and go as they purchased their cocaine all day and all night. The big buyers would be treated to a sampling right out of the giant pile. Thomas would drag out a "rock" of cocaine from the massive pile and crack it open as if he was cutting a diamond. The story of its origin and quality were described as if you were listening to a reading from a science fiction novelist. To watch these people hang on every word of his bullshit was sickening to me. Their wild eyes and grinding jaws were just the physical part of their bizarre behavior. People would hover next to windows, peeking out every few seconds, check the locks on the same doors over and over again as their paranoia increased with every line they snorted.

There was no deterring Thomas from his occupation, as he believed himself invincible—as all drug dealers do. I had watched other old friends get hauled off to jail and I didn't want the same for my brother. One afternoon, I called Thomas and a strange voice picked up the phone. I asked for Thomas and the person on the phone said, "He is unavailable right now, but tell me what you want and I will get it ready for you to pick up." It was obviously a cop, and I knew my brother was probably sitting there in handcuffs while they set up every idiot who called for drugs, then collected them like goldfish as they swam into the net. I called my mother and told her I thought Thomas had been busted. Time would confirm he had. Everyone knew what he was doing, including my mother, but she just didn't want to admit it to herself, and there was nothing she could do to stop it anyway. Later, I watched the evening news and saw reporters standing outside Thomas's house announcing a record cocaine bust. Thomas was sentenced to several years in a federal penitentiary in Texas. He would have spent far more time if he hadn't set up his dealer, who was an even bigger fish in the drug world.

One of the hardest things I have ever done is accompany my mother to Texas to visit her son, my brother Thomas, in prison. Over the years I have seen her strive to survive situations no person should ever be subjected to, but this visit crushed her. The plane ride there was difficult and we spoke very little. The town was a dump of cheap motels and crappy food joints tailored towards the needs of those who visited convicted criminals in this maximum-security prison. Walking her through the doors as they searched us both was humiliating. I couldn't take my eyes off of my mother as the event itself seemed to drain the life out of her. We visited Thomas just the one day and although he physically looked fine, he was an inmate in a sea of prison issue clothing surrounded by armed guards behind tall razor wire fences. I will never forget that moment in my life.

At barely twenty-two years old, I was convinced that my life was ruined. I was moving back to Sacramento from Lake Tahoe after losing my business and my fiancée Karen to my cocaine-snorting partner and former best friend, Pete. It was 1981 and by that time in my short life I had experienced more than most fifty year olds. For one, I had lived on my own since I was fifteen. I didn't have any choice after the abuse I had endured. As far back as I could remember everything seemed to go wrong for me and I was fighting an uphill battle. I put myself through my last years of high school, had no college education, almost everyone I knew abused drugs; I had essentially raised myself from puberty and I obviously didn't know what I was doing. I had made far more mistakes than my ego would allow me to acknowledge. I guess this was my bottom.

Moving back to Sacramento would be the first time in many years I would live with my mom, who had recently become a widow. She needed my help sorting things out, because she was left with a lot of complex issues after Dino's suspicious death.

The story goes that Dino was at an associate's home helping him cut some hedges. He cut into a bush that apparently had a yellow jacket nest in it and they swarmed him and stung him to death. Nobody else at the event was stung, but he was stung several hundred times. The venom in such a massive dose poisoned him, so the story goes. I do believe in Karma (well, I do now!) and the world is a better place without this man, but I don't know if I believe that story. However he died though, this man was in pain, and somehow that feels like vindication for my years of suffering at his hands. I felt horrible for my little brother Harry who was ten years old at the time, because they were so close. I also felt bad for his aging father (my Greek grandpa) who was very ill, as this was his only son and his namesake.

Dino's funeral could be a book in itself. On the day of the funeral, we went from church, to viewing, to church, to graveyard, always with another sermon or eulogy, with unbelievable crying and hysterics. I was in the family limo with my mother, my brothers and poor old Grandpa (Dino's father). Before I got in the limousine, a man walked up to me and introduced himself as Grandpa's doctor. He handed me a bottle of small white pills and told me they were nitroglycerine tablets and to get one under the old man's tongue if he seemed to be having a heart attack. Great, Grandpa is rambling in Greek and may die on my watch! At least Dino is not here to beat me if I fuck this up.

So in the limo I'm tossing these little white pills in Grandpa's mouth like candy. I have no idea what I am doing, but he is still alive and rambling away in Greek. As the limo drives from location to location for this funeral-a-thon, my little brother Harry is watching a helicopter above us. At first, it is a welcome distraction, but the chopper keeps showing up. We see it through the limo's glass sunroof, then notice it when we are getting in and out of limo. The longer this goes on it becomes an obsession for all of us (except Grandpa who is likely about to overdose on little white pills which have the name of an explosive!) At the gravesite ceremony, thank goodness, that frickin' helicopter we have all been obsessing about is not anywhere to be seen. Our limo pulls up followed by a stream of limos and cars. A large tent is up over the gravesite and rows of chairs for the service. The massive flower arrangements, which have somehow followed us from every location, are front and center next to a podium where people will once again speak to what a wonderful father, son, brother, (criminal), blah blah blah Dino was. Everyone is seated and the service is ready to begin.

Defining Moments

Once the sermon begins, though, guess what is back? Yep, we can hear the helicopter, but we can't see it through trees and tent. The noise gets louder and louder and it suddenly drops down behind the podium. The wind from the swirling blades intensifies and the flower displays that sit on tripods start to fall forward and the tent begins to rattle and shake. The wind starts to uproot the tent from the stakes which anchor it. The helicopter is facing us and begins to slowly maneuver to expose its side. The tent is ripped from the ground and tumbles away leaving a clear view of the black helicopter that is lowering itself closer to the ground. The helicopter is about thirty feet above the ground, and now just behind the podium, over the limos. The side door slides open revealing two men in black suits. Everyone starts to dive for cover. I was seated next to Grandpa but I am now flat on the ground with the rest of the crowd attempting to duck the flying flowers, tripods, and debris, expecting a shower of bullets. Chairs are scattering as they tip over and who knows what those two men in the helicopter are going to do?

I look up and the only man standing is Grandpa who has his arms in the air as the wind from the copter pounds him and ripples his suit like a flag in the wind. This deeply religious (and senile) old man proclaims loudly "the lord has come to take my son!" and he continues to repeat this line as if he is a TV preacher in a revival tent. I have an eye on the copter and a hand on Grandpa's leg and am attempting to pull him to the ground with the rest of us. People are barely audible, but they are screaming and crying and in total panic. The men reach inside the helicopter and they hold what appear to be large boxes. They turn the boxes over in all this mayhem; something dumps out in large clumps banging down on the top of the cars and limos they hover over. The loud bangs cause those who aren't looking to think they are explosions or gunfire. A closer look at these clumps reveals that they are flowers! In a misguided effort to sprinkle flowers over the gravesite ceremony, they have terrified everyone (except Grandpa). Most of the crowd starts to realize what is actually happening. The door of the helicopter slides shut and it rises into the air above crowds who lie on their bellies or who have taken off running through the cemetery but one old man, who remains standing with his arms still raised. The crowd begins to rise and a collective chuckle begins to infect the crowd as we all realize what we have just experienced. I am not making this shit up!

In the aftermath of this circus funeral, my mother discovered that Dino had borrowed (or conned) a great deal of money from his father, and Dino's siblings were angry and wanted it repaid by my mother. The Greek family rumor was that my mother was sitting on a stash of smuggled diamonds and should sell them and repay the loan. There were no such diamonds and there was no money. Anyone who owed Dino money disappeared into thin air or claimed they had repaid him. My mother was also left bearing the responsibility of a huge IRS tax lien and a mountain of bills. Mom and eleven year-old Harry were losing everything to the IRS, and it was just a matter of time before they were broke and homeless.

I went home to help her. After all, I had nowhere else to be.

Defining Moments

Chapter 10: A Vision Appears

There is such a thing as love at first sight. I know because it happened to me. Valentine's Day, 1981, I decided to go to this local pick-up joint with Bill and hang with the rest of the hounds. This club, called "The Phone Company," had phones on every table surrounding a dance floor. Each table had a number posted on a short pole that protruded above the phone. Pick up the phone at any table, dial the two digit number of the table you wanted to connect with and there you have it: a coward's way of asking a lady to dance or talk without getting shot down tableside. What can I say? This was the style at the time. I was sitting at the bar with Bill, just a twenty-two year old kid, when a vision walked in. She stopped just a few steps inside the door. She wore purple high waist pants and a cream colored blouse that went all the way to her neckline with ruffled edges framing her stunning face. Her long blond hair flowed down to her shoulders. If I could put a caption over her head, it would have read, "If you talk to me, I will kill you." She looked completely out of place, and her blue eyes lit up the room. Her silent stare suggested that she was not there to be picked up or even approached. She was not the typical girl entering an 80's bar and dance club. My mouth must have dropped open as I watched her every move; she appeared to be looking for someone in particular.

I looked at my friend Bill and I swear I said to him: "I am going to marry that girl!" We hadn't been there long, and I wasn't drunk or impaired in any way, I just remember she seemed to be literally glowing, and I knew. I had never felt this before and I have never felt it since. Bill jokingly picked up a coin from the change on the bar and said "I'll flip you for her" to which I replied, "Flip all you want, that is going to be my wife!" Bill flipped the coin anyway and I called "tails," and tails it was. I had no choice but to muster the courage to talk to her. Her reception was cool.

Her name was Lisa and she was there to meet her friend who happened to be dating the bartender (who I knew well) so that was a good angle for me to work. I was doing pretty well getting to know her when a couple of girls I knew (and who I had hit on earlier) decided to have a little fun and disrupt my progress with this stunning lady. The two girls leaned in, their long dark hair flowing down and draping over each of my shoulders. They began whispering some very descriptive suggestions in my ears as they stroked their fingers through my hair. I can dual task with the best of them, but the offer I was getting in my ears conflicted with the vision across the table. I didn't take my eyes off of Lisa but that wasn't enough to keep the target of my affections seated while I was being propositioned by two beautiful brunettes. Lisa stood abruptly, looked rightfully angry and simply said, "It looks like you are busy," and walked away. I thought my chances of getting her phone number were gone forever as she gathered up her girlfriend and left. Well, I did have "two birds in the hand" and it was Valentine's Day so I managed to do with what I had and I just needed to find a way to track my future wife down . . . later. I did talk to my mother the next morning and told her that I had met the woman I was going to marry—and it wasn't either of the two brunettes in my bed. Gimme a break, it was the eighties!

The bartender made a call for me to his girlfriend in an attempt to get my dream girl's number. I knew it wouldn't be easy because as it turns out she knew of me through high school and my reputation preceded me. Would this "good girl" give her number to a "bad boy?" The ploy worked and somehow Lisa agreed to let me call her.

Lisa had been dating a guy for years and I knew of him. He had attended our high school and he was the quarterback of the football team (my polar opposite). She had only come to the club the night I met her because she was angry with her boyfriend because he chose to spend Valentine's Day with his brother playing basketball (take notes boys). She had called a friend who told her she could get her into this bar because she knew the bartender and they were both under legal drinking age. Lisa was twenty. She was a "good girl" and hadn't ever done anything like that. She had no intention of breaking up with her boyfriend. I looked her square in her beautiful blue eyes and I told her flatly, "You are going to fall so in love with me that you will not even remember this guy's name!"

We were married three years later. After all the years we have been married, I still think of that moment I saw her walk into that bar whenever we are having a tough time. It puts all my love right back where it belongs and nothing else matters.

Chapter 11: The Prescription

Startled, I scan across the windshield and fumble for the ringing crack-berry. It is Ashley and Steve, the drug dealers. Ashley says they are on their way. She tells me how they are having some difficulty raising the cash and are trying to work it out. Ashley takes my temperature on fronting her some of the drugs if they can't get all the cash, and I can hear Steve coaching her in the background. I tell her this is unacceptable. She says she'll get all the money and see me shortly. What will happen next with these flakes? Do they intend on solving their cash problem by robbing me? Will I be pistol whipped, threatened, or shot? I'm not some stoned teenager in Waikiki. I'm too old for this shit.

The minutes click. I just want to live through this and see my wife and children again. Lisa must be thinking all kinds of things, as, being wired, I cannot call her to give her an update. I love her so much, and I always return in my mind to the day I met her and then everything is in perspective and nothing else matters but our love.

Defining Moments

Chapter 12: Who's Your Daddy

Lisa and I discovered "we" were pregnant about four months into our marriage. Even though we had not planned to start a family so early, we were thrilled, excited and anxious at the thought of creating a life conceived by the two of us.

After passing out during the movie at the birthing class, (yes, really!) I was not convinced I was going to be the pillar of strength my wife would need during the birth of our child (and neither was Lisa). I remember the movie; it was titled "The Brazilian Squatting Method." Until then, *The Exorcist* was the scariest movie I had ever seen, and this beat it hands down. I excused myself from the room—which was filled with couples huddled together on little mats on the ground—as I began to pass out. I headed down the hall towards the men's restroom and I felt myself weakening with every step. I pushed on the door and then the next thing I knew, I was waking up on the floor with the restroom door against my side, propping it open like a bag of sand, half of my body in the restroom and half out in the hall. After splashing some water in my face I returned as if nothing had happened, but I knew and I suspected that Lisa did too.

Shortly thereafter, we entered the hospital in first time frantic labor. We were calmly directed to the "birthing room." There was no turning back. There is no way to describe this to anyone who has not witnessed a birth. Those that have, know exactly what I am saying. When my boy let out his first cry, I was so relieved and amazed. He was perfect. A boy. My boy. Brandon. And he had all his fingers and all his toes, and he let out a bellow so excruciating it could curdle milk.

Many changes, challenges and compromises in our marriage would soon follow. Many difficult times required me to recall the moment I first saw Lisa. A second son, Bryce, was added to our family two years later. I have tried to explain to my friends with no children yet that having children changes everything suddenly. Every day, sometimes every second, delivers a new challenge. As much as they want me to tell them what to expect, I cannot prepare them, as no one could have ever prepared me. I have told my friends to imagine driving down a beautiful highway on the way to a vacation spot in the mountains, with all of your plans for the trip clearly in your mind. Now imagine that your car's emergency brake is unexpectedly pulled—hard—your calm drive is suddenly spinning out of control. You don't know which way to turn the wheel or what pedal to push. You just act and react and pray for the best all within a moment. And the car never regains control. That's parenting.

Chapter 13: Fatherhood 101

I had always promised myself I would do everything to be the father I never had. Sometimes you learn what to do from your experiences, and sometimes you learn what not to do. I had learned a lot of what not to do. My experience with my stepfather Dino was a nightmare itself, and then Richard wound up being real trouble. My mother had tried to warn me, but I wanted and needed to know for myself. My mom's warnings could not deter me, as I was a teenager and we all know teenagers are smarter than everyone else. I have a theory about teenagers; basically they could be walking off a cliff towards a canyon and you could yell and scream warnings all you want but your time would be better spent packing them a lunch so they could eat it on the way down. Numerous attempts to let Richard in our lives always ended in disaster. I know it is natural to want to know who your father is. Unfortunately, sometimes he is a complete jerk.

Richard is just not a good person; actually he is quite the opposite. It was difficult for me to discover that my father's lifelong friends didn't even know he had gone. Besides being an alcoholic his whole life, I found out he was a first rate con-man. He was a womanizer, with a taste for young girls, and a big time loser. When I did try to let him into our lives, he was verbally abusive to me, my wife and even my children. The final disaster with Richard followed a family vacation. Richard invited himself to join our annual family beach vacation and I allowed it. Richard was to watch the kids, including my two boys and his boy and girl from a subsequent marriage, one night. They were all in about the same nine to twelve age range. My wife and I wanted to have a dinner alone and Richard didn't seem to mind. When we returned from dinner we discovered that he drove all of the children in his car while he drank Vodka straight from a bottle. Once back at the beach house, he was drunk and he verbally abused my children to the point of terror. I was done. I will never see him again. I believe being a "father" and a "sperm donor" are not at all one in the same.

Defining Moments

The years of my early fatherhood brought more lessons and experiences than I can share. We learned how to raise an eight year old when Brandon turned eight. We learned again how to raise an eight year old when Bryce turned eight. You get where I am going with this. I always found it ignorant when someone would advise me how to raise my child when they had no children at all or they had children younger than mine. The most absurd statements begin with the words "my children will never." I never offered advice to any parent, and I never welcomed a statement about raising my children that began with the words "you should."

I have always tried to be the best dad I could be, because it was up to me to make their upbringing different than mine. I coached their soccer, baseball and football teams for many seasons. I walked my boys to school, helped with their homework (as much as I could) and I tried to be an important part of their lives as well as a positive influence. As I continued to succeed in business, our lifestyle improved. Throughout their childhoods, we've had a good life and a beautiful home, nice cars, good communities, and the best of schools. I encouraged their interests by making sure they had the equipment they needed to pursue them. For instance, when Brandon showed a real interest in and talent for photography, he received his dream camera for Christmas. I have loved my wife and I have shown my children that I love them. The boys have witnessed firsthand what a healthy spousal relationship is and that was something I never saw in my childhood home. I always believed in teaching my children to respect all people in all walks of life. On the holidays I sent my boys out to give freshly baked cookies to the people who collected our garbage. I taught the boys how to care for our yard, mowing and edging, and they had household responsibilities and chores (and I never sprayed them with a hose nozzle, at least not to compel yard work). I believed they needed to learn good strong work ethics. But I never once hit them, and I never abused them, as I had learned "what not to do" as a father. I did everything I could think of to give them the best chance to succeed in life.

I protected them from what I felt were bad influences, including, sadly, my brother, their Uncle Thomas, who had not been reformed in prison. He was an addict, and into horse racing. When my boys were in grammar school, our neighbor asked me who the man was who came to our home during the day while we were at work. He said that this guy, sometimes with another man, would enter our house through the garage with the keypad code. We knew nothing of this! The neighbor described the car, and the description matched Thomas's car. I showed him a family photo and he identified Thomas as the guy. When I searched my house I found liquid Hydrocodone prescribed for horses. Thomas had been using my house as his daytime drug den. When I confronted him, he denied it, and even went so far as to blame Brandon and Bryce. He threw his nephews under the bus to cover his ass. Another rift between us. I had to protect my boys.

In their teenage years, Brandon and Bryce were as different as perfect strangers, and they were becoming young men. As they began to become more independent from me and from each other, they became interested in different things. I tried to accommodate them as individuals and stay close to them. I tried my damndest to embrace each son and his hobbies and desires equally.

Bryce began to love golf, so we played golf often and eventually joined a country club so he could play as often as he liked. In the summer, he would spend entire days at the club, soon becoming a great golfer and playing four years on his high school team. He also learned what I call "accidental etiquette" which was my pet phrase for his learning great manners around adults as he golfed with them. A kind of "wax-on wax-off"-*Karate Kid*-subliminal learning, similar to how I learned to fight. Some of my fondest memories are of the days I got to watch him golf competitively. Such a fine young man and a great sport; win or lose, he shows class and dignity.

Brandon eventually lost his interest in youth sports and had no interest in golf. He did, however, love hot rods. He was intrigued by my high school hot rod, so we found the same make, model and year of car in horrible condition. The only positive comment Lisa could make was, "at least it runs." I taught both of my boys to drive a stick shift on this beat up Chevelle before my eldest and I began to take it completely apart in an attempt to restore this classic car to its original condition with a hot rod twist. The deeper we dug into it, the more rust and damage we found. There were so many holes rusted through the bottom we could see the garage floor through the trunk. We removed every wire, rubber seal, window felt, and had boxes full of zip-lock baggies that were marked with a Sharpie what the part was and where it had come from. When Brandon was about fifteen, we went to Hot August Nights in Reno, a huge hot rod auto show. We wandered through these aisles of incredible cherry vehicles and talked about how someday ours could be alongside these beauties.

This project would prove to be a huge challenge that would last seven-plus years, partly because it coincided with the start of Brandon's drug use. What started as a project he was very enthusiastic about became an afterthought to time with friends and partying. He would show up for certain monumental events like when we put the body back on the frame after it was painted, but I was pretty much on my own with it for a bit. My wife was a champ as "that thing" (her nick-name for it) sat in a million pieces in the garage for so long.

Seeing Brandon heading down the wrong path, I knew only what not to do. I had no idea what to do.

I remember a lesson I learned while coaching youth sports. "The hardest kid to coach is your own." A true statement. I found myself unable to dissuade my eldest son from the dangerous road he would travel.

Chapter 14: What Have I Done Wrong

When Brandon was about eighteen, I busted him for being stoned. I knew the way pot smelled, so it wasn't any great detective work that led me to it. Soon after this, we discovered he had obtained a license to obtain medical marijuana. I was surprised. Turns out, it's legal for my child (and yours) to buy, possess and grow pot and the only requirement is that they want it!

Any little shithead can get a "medical" license to smoke marijuana in California when he turns eighteen. In fact, it's a rite of passage, even more than a drivers' license nowadays. The students hand around a list of unscrupulous doctors who are willing to do a consultation for a fee and then write a prescription for a fee so your child can go to some legal dope dispensary and buy all the "sticky-icky green bud" he or she wants. They don't need a parent to sign, they just need to recite from a passed-around list of symptoms as to why they need this marijuana when they show up to this farce of a doctor's appointment.

Apparently half of the high school has obtained this license to smoke pot and can buy the strongest pot available, legally.

I went and got one for myself—as an experiment—and was astonished at how easy it was. In the waiting room at the doctor's office I had thirty years on every single person. I also felt like I must have been the only one gainfully employed, well-groomed, thoughtfully dressed. It was an insane experience.

This law has been sold to voters by showing cancer patients and other sick people who need this drug to ease symptoms, but the teenagers of the state have exploited this, now that it is law. When I went from the "doctor" to the dispensary, I didn't see any of the sad beneficiaries they always show on television; the handicapped and sickly were nowhere to be seen. It actually resembled a fraternity party, except for the glass cases displaying an array of pot labeled with colorful names, potency and detailed descriptions, which read like something on the back of a wine label: The "Orange Crush" had "hints of berry with a smooth finish." That is about as far as I got into the room before my presence stuck out like a parent at a kegger party. I was by far the oldest guy in the room. I was approached and asked for my license, which, of course, I showed. I was given the grand tour and a detailed break down of how each different bud worked better for different symptoms. This one is for sleeplessness, this one for appetite stimulation, this one for back pain, and this one—believe it or not—is for asthma. It was absurd.

I know there are people out there who claim they need this drug, but those people were not my son or half of the high school, nor did anyone at this dispensary seem to be suffering from anything but red, squinty eyes.

But, we thought, at least our son is only smoking legal pot. I did it, and I'm okay.

As time went on Brandon was showing signs that he was faltering. I busted him again. Then, he began to collect speeding tickets, show up to work on the Chevelle apparently inebriated, fight with his brother, be non-participatory in the family. As I have freely admitted, I experimented with drugs in the seventies and the eighties and was no stranger to the signs of his drug use or the possibility of drug dealing. I knew all too well what could be ahead if he didn't change his lifestyle. I had lost a couple of close friends to drug overdoses and a couple I knew were in prison. My own older brother had been sent to prison for drug dealing and although he had long been free from incarceration, he will never be free from his issues surrounding addiction. My biological father is an alcoholic, refusing to acknowledge his addiction and destroying any chance of being part of my youth or my children's (his grandchildren's) lives. Watching drugs tear apart my family and kill my friends had sent me in the opposite direction as an adult, as a husband and as a father.

Soon Lisa and I couldn't ignore Brandon's behavior. That it would just go away, or that he would grow out of it like I did didn't seem likely. His grades were terrible, and he kept getting in trouble for being in the wrong place at the wrong time or with the wrong person. For instance, he was put on probation for being in a car with someone who was in possession of a replica firearm. He looked like total shit, and when we confronted him about it, he was feeling bad enough that he confessed: He was addicted to the pain pill known as Oxy. He told us that he needed our help to get off of it.

We never thought to find the reasoning behind the drug abuse, we just thought he had tried it and grew to feel dependent on it. He was always a tough kid to raise and he was often a handful and we felt this problem could be handled like any other. But we were novices when it came to helping someone kick drug addiction.

We did our best to assist him and we attempted to detox him at home. We called Brandon's real doctor (not the ones who prescribe marijuana) and asked for guidance. We tried to keep him away from everyone we knew until we could get the drugs out of his system.

We told no one.

It needed to be our immediate family's dirty little secret.

Thomas and I had fallen out because of his continued preference for drugs and that lifestyle and an inclination toward our biological father's proclivity for untruths and big scams. The last thing I wanted was for Thomas to be a part of this. Oh, how he would rub my face in this shit.

You would think with all my experience around drugs that I would have known what to do. That is exactly what I thought! Brandon was sickly and skinny. My wife lay with him for hours rubbing his back and keeping fluids in him. He went from cold to hot and back again. In a couple of weeks he was looking much healthier and we sent him out into the world again.

Turns out, just because I did drugs and knew people who were addicted to drugs I was still not qualified to understand how to break someone from craving the drugs that satisfy their addiction. Brandon seemed better and we thought we had helped him simply because we incarcerated him at home away from his peers until he had the drugs out of his system. In our mind, he was cured.

Unfortunately, the problem had not been solved so easily. Like any good movie, this solution came too easily and too early in the drama. He was such a child then, easily influenced and dealing with challenges in counterproductive ways. He was caught being truant, being out past curfew, being with a kid who stole a wallet. He was involved in multiple car accidents. Brandon struggled and was barely making it through high school, so we changed him to a problem-child school to enable him to graduate. He and his younger brother Bryce were growing apart just as I had grown apart from my brother Thomas, which was torturous for me and Lisa to watch. Brandon dressed like some punk and believed he was the smartest person in the room. He became a very obnoxious person.

At some point, we knew he was back into drugs, we just hoped he wasn't getting himself addicted. We were kidding ourselves. We felt so powerless. He was gaunt, broken out, nervous and angry, telling random stories that always involved the biggest-fastest-shortest-longest-cue-the-orchestra-everybody fucking him over. He'd always have to go save someone in some dramatic fashion.

The things that would come out of his mouth were completely unbelievable lies and his ignorance was evident to all. As a parent, I was humiliated when Brandon spoke. We encouraged him to seek help, but as an adult Brandon had to want help and he had to consent to help. The thought of Brandon being addicted to drugs, overdosing, getting arrested was all too torturous to contemplate, but we did it anyway. How could we not? He was our son.

I was so angry at Brandon at one point that I stood with a hammer over the Chevelle and considered destroying it. The Chevelle sitting unfinished in the garage had become a grim symbol of the disappointment I felt with my son. Instead, I arranged to have it towed to a friend's shop with the agreement that Brandon and I would show up together twice a week and work towards finishing the project with the assistance of a professional (and the expectations of someone other than Dad). It didn't work to bring Brandon back.

I warned and warned, but no matter how much I warned him, he continued his journey to the dark side. He was over six feet tall and weighed less than 140 pounds. He was sickly, late to every family event and completely high when and if he showed up. He was a constant embarrassment at large family gatherings as he was the last to show and the first to go. When our Chevelle was ready for its maiden voyage, he was a no show. I delayed starting the car for hours, expecting he might be late, but he never showed. That car started for the first time since I had taught the boys to drive, and Brandon missed this moment because drugs were now more important to him than anything or anybody.

I looked at photos of Brandon growing up and wondered if I would view them in a slideshow at his funeral. My marriage suffered because Lisa defended Brandon vehemently. I completely understood, because I had grown up with a similar scenario: my mother's unwillingness to see Thomas's problem. My wife and I had many confrontations, and while we both knew he had a problem, we disagreed on the severity and the solution.

Soon, Brandon moved in with his girlfriend, Tiffanie, and she was as strung out as he was. When they were together, they looked like two skeletons embracing. They had grown fuzzy around their edges; it's difficult to describe how they clung to each other in a desperate way as if they didn't know where one ended and the other began. It was more than teenage passion driving them to that; it was dependence, an unhealthy co-dependence. They couldn't meet anyone's eyes; their pinpoint pupils darted around the room when I spoke to them. They couldn't answer simple questions coherently. They babbled and told those outrageous stories. They were sick.

When my wife and I heard sirens or the phone rang late at night, we always thought the worst. Certain police or crime television shows would give us lumps in our throats as we would silently look at each other and know we were thinking the same thing ... that might be our son.

One afternoon while I was at work, Lisa was trying to help Brandon out by organizing some of his bills. Brandon told her that he needed to run a quick errand. She called me later that day and said she had lost track of him and he wasn't returning her calls or answering his phone. All the usual horrible thoughts began to surface in our minds. The day turned into night and we still hadn't heard from him. Close to midnight, as Lisa and I watched a movie together in the dark, there was a loud banging at our back sliding glass door. Our dogs went crazy—they were as startled as we were. Who the fuck was at our back door? It was Brandon's druggie friend, high as a kite, rambling a mile a minute. What would possess him to go to the backdoor and not the front but being high and thus, stupid.

Brandon had been arrested, he told us, in a set-up drug sting. He was in the local jail and had been calling friends to bail him out. Our son hadn't called us for bail; I had told him that he shouldn't bother me when he got busted, one thing I had said that had apparently sunk in to his thick head.

Defining Moments

He was alive—a relief—but we had no idea how much trouble he was in. The thoughts of trial and incarceration were unthinkable, but they were likely. The memory of accompanying my mother half way across the country to visit my brother in jail came back strong. I called the jail and received minimal information beyond his bail amount. We opted to leave Brandon in jail. He was released twenty-three hours later on his own recognizance.

Brandon spent the days after his release from jail back at our home as we attempted the daunting task of detoxing him. Through withdrawals again! Brandon became sicker every day that his frail body went without the Oxy it craved to survive. Brandon had lived away from our house for over a year and he looked like a ghost of himself. His eyes were dark, his enthusiastic personality was gone and his mind seemed permanently altered. He was twenty-three years old, 6' 2" and his weight was hovering at a skeletal 130 pounds.

We had Brandon on complete lockdown at our house with no visitors allowed, searching his room and the entire house daily. We ordered professional quality drug tests so we could test him every day. Brandon experienced the worst of the drug withdrawals in the first few days after his arrest. My wife, Lisa, sat on the bathroom floor with him during his lowest moments. He vomited until he had nothing left. He curled up in the fetal position, chanting inaudible ramblings and contorting to the point that we had to pad the doorframe and cabinets with towels to keep him from banging his head and limbs.

In the twelfth hour of fetal position rocking, infantile whimpering, sickening dry heaves and panicked breathing, I broke out my video camera, thinking I'd just tape a reminder: He can't possibly ever want to do this again. His mother on the bathroom floor alongside him, cushioning his head before it smacks the doorframe, stroking his back and newly shorn hair. I am defined again by this moment, disgusted by myself, but in a warped way triumphant: You see, you see you little shit—what happens when you don't listen to me? He was a walking skeleton and you could see his every rib. The bones on his spine looked like a row of knots stretched under his skin. His pelvic bones stuck out reminiscent of a dead animal's carcass on the roadside. He looked like one of the horrid pictures you see of a concentration camp victim. Oxy is considered synthetic heroin, and sometimes referred to as "hillbilly heroin," as powerful and addictive a drug as you will find anywhere on the street.

Children, however, never learn from their parents' I-told-you-sos. He was like a sick animal and we just tried to keep fluids in him and listen to the doctors who guided our effort. After the initial detox period, we used professional grade drug tests and surprised him with them. He always had an excuse for why he couldn't pee. I would hand him a bottle of water and tell him I would wait. He was never truly clean.

When he slept, I went into the bedroom to see if his chest was inflating with air to assure me he was still alive. It reminded me of when our boys were babies and sometimes we would check on them in the night or as they napped and we never left the room until we verified they were breathing just because that is what a parent does.

Defining Moments

Chapter 15: Happy Frickin' Holidays

As Thanksgiving approached, our traditions looked impossible to pull off. We were evasive when we called my wife's parents to tell them not to come to our house as they usually did. We said we had some personal family issues to deal with. We could tell their feelings were hurt, but we didn't feel we had any other choice. We did allow my younger brother Harry in on the whole awful situation and invited him to come to the house as planned. I needed my younger brother because he had developed a great relationship with my boys. He's eleven years younger than me, and in the music business where he works shooting videos for rap artists my sons listen to. He'd had a solid relationship with both of our boys, and that could translate into communication.

This Thanksgiving we had an agenda that didn't include turkey and all the trimmings.

Agenda Item One: Get our son's belongings out of his rental house. The landlord met me, Lisa, Harry, Harry's wife Anabel, and a shaking miserable Brandon at the house, and I felt sorry for the owner of this home. He was a deeply religious man accompanied by his mousy wife and perfectly groomed daughter, all dressed in their Sunday best on their way home from church. He had believed all of Brandon's lies, trusted my son and his roommates and ended up landlord of a drug den. He was devastated to see the condition of his property but he was strangely calm and understanding. He simply wanted our help to get Brandon's belongings out of his house and fix things as best we could. He gave us an offer we couldn't refuse. If we would get everything out by the evening and pull out all of the carpet, he would not pursue damages.

None of us were prepared for what we saw when we turned the key in the lock and opened the door. Paper and cardboard blackened the windows. When we removed these window covers, we found broken panes behind them. The bedroom doors had been kicked in, and broken bongs and stem pipes, empty cigarette packs, matchbooks, just trash littered every surface. I don't know what the hell these people (my son!) did in here, but the carpet could not have been dirtier if they raised farm animals indoors. Pictures of Brandon and his friends holding automatic weapons were nearly the only things upright. Sex toys filled the drawers and around his bed. Apparently, it had been a real bohemian festival at some point, at least to the people who hung here.

Everything was broken or ajar, apparently ransacked while Brandon was in jail. Nearly all of his belongings that were worth anything were stolen by the scumbags who had been his peers. We heard Brandon's girlfriend, Tiffanie, was afraid to return to the house while our son was in jail and it was probably the smartest thing she had done in years. Brandon had accumulated flat screen TV's, computers, stereo equipment, guns, you name it and it was all gone. Most of it, if not all of it was drug trade merchandise or purchased with drug sale money before his drug habit escalated to the point that his addiction was larger than he could support with his sales. The area under the rental house had been dug out and reinforced to grow indoor marijuana. It resembled an escape tunnel from a prison movie. None of this was intended for the eyes of a parent.

I don't believe mine or Thomas's place ever looked half as bad, but if I could see the boxing ring, mismatched couches and the hanging roach clip from where I stand now, who knows what it would look like to me.

We spent the next twelve hours cleaning, hauling and tossing. We rented a local storage unit and brought the furniture and clothes there but we tossed out more than we took. We filled nearly fifty large black garbage bags of filth and drug paraphernalia and left them for trash pickup in the alley behind the house. Most things of value had been stolen or pawned. One of these things was the expensive camera we had given him for Christmas. It was at the pawnshop.

Agenda Item Two: Retrieve valuables from the pawnshop. The camera was sitting at a local pawnshop as collateral on a loan that expired on the very day we got there for it. It was the first time I had ever stepped foot in a pawnshop; it was a shit hole covered with other people's Christmas and birthday presents. It was humiliating for me to be in this place, and my son could not look me in the eyes the entire time we were there. The walls were lined with guitars. The glass counters held cameras, jewelry and trinkets of all types. The floors and shelves were covered with tools and equipment. The stuff was busting out of the place. The people who ran it were the lowest form of life, preying on the weak, broke and addicted. My son produced a crumpled receipt and for a couple hundred dollars we reclaimed his dream camera. I thought this camera meant the world to him. The camera was apparently second and last to his need for drugs—duh—like everything else. I knew I couldn't be the first parent who paid off the loan on a child's prized belongings. I did know that it would remain my camera until he could pay back everything he owed and prove to me he was sober. It broke my heart that I was retrieving something from hock that we had given him as the perfect gift to inspire him, and that it had ended up helping fund his drug habit. It broke my heart that my Brandon was a drug addict.

Agenda Item Three: Confront Brandon directly with an intervention. The family intervention included me, Bryce, Harry, Anabel, Lisa and even the arresting officer, Denny White, via phone. The intervention started with the assumption that Brandon was currently detoxing (for the second time) with us at home, and there were expectations everyone had of him. Brandon was attacked by all sides; the room was heated with Brandon's denial and lies. He lied and denied because that is what drug addicts do. Brandon was mistaken thinking that he was smarter than everyone else because while he was the dealer, other people—addicts—hung on his every word as though he was speaking gospel. The person dishing out the drugs rambles stupidly and thinks his admirers should be carving his wise words in a stone tablet. Been there, seen that with Thomas and others!

We had been giving him regular drug tests, which showed levels of positive, and that line had been starting to drop. It seemed to be leaving his system—it took a while to be completely clean.

But at some point during the intervention, in between the crying and the lying, it occurred to me that this boy didn't look like he was suffering the effects of withdrawals. His symptoms seemed to be suddenly better and his detox wasn't as severe as we thought it would be or as bad as it had been the first time years before. And I cocked my head and listened more carefully to his lies—the lies which I suddenly realized were consistent with his past behavior when he was high. Stop the presses!

I sprung up and shook my finger in the air in front of his face.

"Are you high right now, Brandon?"

"Nah." He looked at his Nikes.

"When was the last time you took Oxy?"

No response. Brandon shuffled his feet and stretched his spine, scratched the corner of his eye, but as is consistent with his behavior, continued to lie and deny.

I am shaking my arms and getting down in Brandon's face. I am shouting at his face. I am screaming at the shell of my firstborn.

"Are you high? Are you high right now?" Spittle lands on his face; he blinks but does not flinch.

"Bryce, go search your brother's room. Now!"

Brandon stood up to leave, but Harry stood up from his dining room chair and went towards him and so did Lisa. They asked Brandon to sit back down on the overstuffed chair and he did.

"He won't find anything in there," Brandon mumbled.

A few minutes later, Bryce rounded the corner into the room with his arms outstretched cupping the Oxy and foil he found inside CD cases. I had never even thought to check there. Brandon stood up. Bryce glared into Brandon's eyes, and in the room's dead silence Bryce laid the drugs and the burned black-sketched foil on the counter like it was a dead animal.

I stood in front of Brandon, looking slightly up at him, as he is taller than me. The room was silent and everyone awestruck. After what we just went through with him... I looked Brandon in his guilty darkened eyes and I said, "Prepare yourself to find out what will happen to you every time you lie to me . . . are you ready?"

Before he could reply or even contemplate my words, I felt the crack of Brandon's nose on my knuckles and he flew backwards off his feet. My family's loud simultaneous gasps accompanied Harry and Bryce's rush to restrain me as if I was going to continue the beating. Maybe kill Brandon. This is how angry we all were. How out of our element. And now I'd done it.

Lisa jumped up screaming and crying and yelled, "Stop!" Brandon lay face down and his blood soaked the carpet beneath his head. His hands clutched his face. He moaned and rolled over. Blood oozed from between his clenched fingers and ran down his chest when he sat up. My wife was hysterical and rightfully so. I stood there numb, wondering what I had done and how did my efforts to be the best father I could be turn into this? I'd hit him—once. But I intended to never hit my child. I had promised myself I would never, ever repeat this offense I had endured as a child.

I just wanted to slap him out of it, to hurt him as we were hurting, because he seemed oblivious to the magnitude of our pain. It all happened so fast and when I realized that Brandon was bringing these drugs into our house, while we thought we were detoxing him, it was beyond me. I felt violated in so many ways, all at once and I snapped. Brandon's nose was broken and my wife and sister-in-law attended to him to stop the bleeding and I sat in silent shock with Harry and Bryce flanking me on the couch— possible guards against any further explosion into violence. There was no threat of that, as this intervention was over. Way over.

The next day things had calmed down, and Brandon admitted to needing professional help, more than we could offer. He had been living on less since he was on lock-down and that was lowering the level in the tests, but he was really never without Oxy.

It was late 2008 and my business was suffering the effects of the economic meltdown. Just a couple of years before that my business income had been five times what it was then. Bryce, in college, was working three jobs to pay his own expenses, something we could no longer afford to help with. Simply put, we were falling behind on everything and we didn't have the money to put Brandon in a rehab. So we began searching the internet for someplace that would take him without an exorbitant amount of cash. The State run agencies were crammed with voluntary admissions and court ordered treatment. Brandon's girlfriend, Tiffanie, had already been in a thirty-day rehab twice before. We had heard plenty of horror stories from her about her stint in the county rehab: Apparently, several people had over-dosed on drugs while in the facility, one had died, and she had relapsed and used Oxy while she was in there. The problem with a facility that accepts court ordered patients is that the patient doesn't want to be there. They are basically given the option of jail or rehab and they make the clear choice. Drugs were as easy to get as a pudding cup inside these places.

We kept shopping for a place that could assure us that we just weren't introducing our son to more drug addicts who would help each other continue their abuse. Every agency we contacted seemed to be selling something, and they were pushy and wanted money transferred to them now, offering to pick Brandon up immediately. We felt like we were buying a used car from some slickster. We didn't have the money for what most of these places cost but we knew he needed their help or he could be just another statistic. This was so far out of our realm of understanding and far from our abilities to negotiate. A maze of tangled claims and questionable results.

Brandon also needed to be available to the narcotics officers to fulfill his end of a bargain he had struck with them during his brief incarceration. We decided to try to detox him as long as it took for him to get his arrangement with the narcotics officers completed, and then we would continue to find a state run program to admit him or reach our hands out to our family, who until now had primarily been kept in the dark. We were desperate for professional help.

Chapter 16: The Law

Brandon had been set up by another drug dealer. This person had called our son from a wired phone while Brandon was with his mother—that so-called errand was a drug deal.

He left his mother to straighten out his bills while he went to do a drug deal. Unbelievable.

He was supposed to bring drugs to a hotel room, but because Brandon owed everybody money, his credit to be fronted drugs was not good, so he went to the drug deal without the drugs, planning to get the money first, then go back for them. When Brandon knocked on the hotel room door, it opened and an army of police officers darting in from all directions greeted him. They wrestled him to the ground, cuffed him and began their search of him and his vehicle and, later, his house. Brandon had been recorded agreeing to the deal and he had paraphernalia in his possession. Unfortunately for the police, they chose to drop the net on him when he had hit bottom and couldn't afford the drugs they hoped they would catch him with.

During his twenty-three hour period in jail, the narcotics officers shook him down for everything he was worth. The process of getting one drug dealer to set up the next is as old as the trade itself (my own brother had done it over thirty-five years before). During the interrogation, which included the usual scare tactics, the cops showed him a great deal of information they had collected on him. Even though they didn't have the bust they wanted, they had him verbally agreeing to provide drugs and several people willing to testify that Brandon had provided them with Oxy and other drugs. They had been monitoring him for some time and had ample surveillance to make up for the lack of drugs at his actual bust. Brandon had been dealing Oxy for the past few years and the police had been looking to get him. Brandon had at one time been moving thousands of these tiny green prescription pain pills through California, making nighttime drives to Los Angeles and back to buy huge quantities to supply the Sacramento area.

They were charging him with three felonies and he was facing five plus years in prison. Faced with the charges, Brandon waved his attorney rights and talked too much—a strung out drug addict who just got popped. The interrogation lasted nearly twenty hours; although, to Brandon, it felt like three days. Looking at the abundance of evidence and the thought of five years in prison, Brandon broke and agreed to bust a dealer named Steve. The interesting thing about Steve was that much of the information the officers had on Brandon was from Steve.

It's quite a tangled web.

Steve had been busted some time ago and was released when he agreed to work with the narcotics division of the police department. Steve's bust was kept a secret so he could fold back into the drug world unnoticed and collect information on drug dealers like my son and share that information with the officers so they could set up these dealers. Steve was tasked with introducing undercover officers into the inner circle that would eventually lead to a bust that appeared to be far removed from the original contact with Steve. The only problem with Steve is that he was double-crossing the narcotics officers and they had come to discover his deception. Steve and his girlfriend, Ashley were highly addicted to Oxy and their combined drug habit made it necessary for him to continue to deal Oxy to the bigger buyers while tossing a few small fish to the officers to appease them and satisfy his deal. The officers knew too that Steve was beating his girlfriend and forcing her to perform "happy ending massages" and sexual favors to support her personal addiction to Oxy. Brandon was one of the small fish that Steve provided information on. Brandon had become so addicted that he could no longer supply the drug in quantity because he and Tiffanie consumed over $1000 a day by snorting or smoking it. Brandon had gone from a large dealer to a junkie who would do anything, say anything and sell anything to get his next fix. Brandon had become dispensable to Steve and the other large dealers, as he was now an Oxy addicted con man in constant search of his next dose of this potent drug.

Brandon could trade prison for setting up the double-crosser Steve. Officer White was insistent that the time frame for this deal was short. Brandon was very ill detoxing, and the fact that he had been busted and he was on lockdown at his parents' house was common knowledge on the street. There's no easy way to bluff if everyone sees your cards.

Officer White cooked up a scheme. He gave Brandon a phone number and a story for him to give to Steve. Hopefully this story would explain Brandon's bust, now known by all of his associates: He was to acknowledge his bust and tell Steve that the cops didn't catch him with drugs because no one would front him the Oxy he was to bring to the deal. Brandon owed everyone, including Steve, so that would not be difficult to believe. In fact, that part was the truth! He was then supposed to tell Steve that he needed help supplying one of his regulars while his parents were holding him with a tight leash and ask him if he could do it. All Brandon was asking for in return for this connection was a few Oxy pills dropped at our house as a referral fee. Brandon asked Steve to just put the pills on his windowsill so he could get high unbeknownst to his parents. The intention was to make Steve believe that Brandon was still using, and thus trustworthy.

Brandon was a nervous wreck. He was completely confused after days of detox and scared to death that he was going to prison if the scheme failed. Brandon contacted the other drug dealer from his own cell phone so Steve would recognize the number. Brandon told Steve the concocted story and then supplied Steve with the phone number that Officer White had given him for the phony buyer. Immediately there was trouble: The officer had accidentally given Brandon the same phone number that Steve already possessed; the same number that had been given to Steve by the same officers for his use when he was setting up a bust of his own. Brandon was outed big time. Our son was immediately labeled a snitch on the street and had no chance of helping the police. Our phone began ringing with crank calls and threats on his life and ours. The officers were apologetic; it was apparently an honest mistake. Since our son couldn't see the deal through, he would be charged with the three felonies. Brandon was facing five years in prison.

I was pissed off that the cops fucked this up! It was the one chance for my firstborn son to avoid prison, and damn-it there had to be another way. It was now time for me to intervene. To pull out whatever stops needed to be pulled to protect him. To save him. My boy. Brandon.

I set an appointment with the arresting officers. I arrived at the police station with Brandon and we were escorted to an interview room. We were sitting in the police station in a county that is known for being tough on drugs and prosecuting everything to the fullest ability of the law. The door opened to a closet-size room with a table and four chairs. The walls were stark white and the room could barely accommodate the meager furnishings. Officer White and his Sergeant entered the room and sat opposite us. They were unrelenting that Brandon owed them a bust, no matter their mistake. My son sat there with me and he was not only very ill, he had an obvious broken nose (about which the officers did not inquire—I know they had their theories) and Brandon was still very addicted to Oxy.

Brandon was smoking these pills at a heavy clip. He had started his habit by taking the pills orally, then snorting them; finally he had escalated to burning them on foil while inhaling the fumes through a stem pipe. Although the next step was slamming or injecting in his veins, he hadn't gone that far. He was up to about thirty Oxy pills a day and couldn't sell enough to supply his habit. While he had been living on less since his home lock-down, he was really never clean during this detox. How was Brandon going to achieve what these cops wanted in his condition and with his new reputation as a snitch?

I am the father, with all that that means. I am the man of the family, and I would do anything to protect my family, but I was in unchartered territory here once again. What would Dino NOT do? What would Richard NOT do?

I looked the undercover narcotics officer in the face and blurted, "I'll do the bust!"

I'm raising my freaking hand like I am volunteering to coach a soccer team. I believe firmly that the deal to bust Steve should be forgiven due to the failure on the part of the police and the complete and total fiasco that had come from the officers not doing their homework and giving Brandon the same number that Steve already knew was an undercover cop's phone. They have pushed me into a corner and I only see one absurd way out.

"We don't let parents work off deals to keep their kids out of prison," Officer White responded after several moments of silent staring around the room.

I didn't plan on volunteering, and I strongly suspected (hoped?) I didn't have a chance in hell at getting the officers to give me the go-ahead. I just said it because a father does whatever he can do to help his son. At least that is what I had always thought and that is what I had always done. Brandon looked at me as if he wanted to stop me but he lacked the clarity to speak, desperation the only thing evident on his weary face. The days since Brandon's arrest had been some of the toughest days of his life.

We know that the practice of turning your busted drug users and dealers into snitches was nothing new in the world of illegal drug distribution. I had consumed my fair share of drugs and wasn't just some innocent bystander. I had my own issues. Maybe this was somehow Karma.

They certainly don't have a book that can teach you how to be a good father, and my own experiences as a son and a stepson had only given me insight on what not to do as a father. Even if this magical book did exist that could help you raise the perfect child, I assume that the chapter titled, "How to Do a Drug Bust for Your Son" would be absent.

I knew Brandon couldn't do this because he was too hot on the streets as a snitch. I pressed the issue, which was met with emphatic refusals each time. The officers continued to hold their ground and refused to agree to work with me.

I pushed: "I don't want you to work with me. I just want to know what you would do if I contacted you and told you that Steve was meeting me to buy one-hundred Oxys? What is your job responsibility in that case?"

"We would do our job if someone called and informed us of a drug deal," Officer White said.

"If I am able to get Steve busted, would that count for my son's deal?" I asked.

The officer and his sergeant left the room for about ten minutes before returning to tell me that it would.

"We are not condoning or encouraging this in any way," Officer White insisted.

That was all I needed.

Now Brandon and I would need to work out the rest.

Defining Moments

Chapter 17: A Father's Devotion

Brandon became my coach: In order to convincingly portray a drug supplier, I had to know the lingo. I had to know the system. I was miles from toot and half an ocean from weed. I would need Brandon to assist me with current drug terms. What did an Oxy look like? What milligram size I should say I have? Brandon told me that the easiest way to buy pills is from people who are prescribed them for chronic pain and intentionally demand more than they need from their doctors so they can resell them at an enormous profit. Brandon told me that the Holy Grail for an Oxy dealer was to find an "old guy with a script" (prescription); so I decided this would be who I would become.

I went to a Wal-Mart and purchased a pre-paid cellular phone that I would use as my undercover phone. I didn't need my last name popping up on a caller I.D. I nicknamed the phone my "crack-berry."

After getting crucial information and doing a bit of research, I found the Craigslist classified advertisement with a picture of a young blond girl offering massages with a contact phone number that matched the drug dealer Steve's number. The pictures in the ad were racy and the price per session was about twice the normal cost for such services. I called to set up a "massage." I told her I got massages often for my ailing back but I thought it would be fun to get a massage from a pretty young lady. We scheduled an appointment for later that same day.

I've had back problems in the past, as many fifty year olds do, so I dug up a back support and I wore it to the appointment. I had a basic plan and an obvious goal but how it would unfold was a mystery. She met me at the door, dressed in casual sweats and no make-up. Despite looking a little weary, she looked like she could be very attractive if she tried. As I looked at her, I felt sorry for her because I knew she was about the same age as my sons, and I knew she was somebody's daughter, somebody's baby, and I also knew the sordid details of her existence. She led me into a surprisingly clean bedroom that had a complete bedroom set and a mirrored closet door was beside the bed. She pointed me towards a chair in the corner of the room and told me

Defining Moments

I could get undressed and put my clothes on the chair. She excused herself, telling me that she was getting a towel to cover the bed where the massage would take place. I thought I could hear her whispering to someone in the apartment, but I only heard her voice. Now I was really wondering what I had walked in to.

I labored to get my shoes off: A well placed moan and groan intended to prompt her curiosity.

"Are you all right?" she asked, coming back into the room with a towel and spreading it flat onto the bed, then bending down and helping me untie my shoes.

"I have back problems," I said, standing to remove my dress shirt, exposing the back brace which I removed with angst.

"Have your doctors given you anything for the pain?" she asked, helping my shirt off of each shoulder.

I told her I had been given many medications, but I needed to be able to work my job so couldn't take most of them.

"I am a Financial Planner and I can't afford to be loopy," I said.

"What kinds of stuff do they give you?" She pooched out her lower lip and tried to look more sad than excited.

The conversation was headed quickly in the direction I had planned. I told her they had given me Vicodin, Darvocet and Oxycodone, which I definitely couldn't tolerate. She was quickly moving towards the hook in this trap.

"What do you do with the drugs if you don't take them?"

"I've probably got one hundred Oxycodone pills in my safe at home with as many refills as I want, but I won't be using them," I said.

"I'll take them if you don't want them."

Fish on!

"I'll bet you would. I had a friend who sold his for a lot of money to a coworker," I said.

I still had my pants on when she offered to buy the Oxy.

I noticed that she had left the door to the bedroom wide open and I wondered if someone was listening. I told her I was a "professional" and a "family man" and it just wasn't worth the risk. She said she understood but if I changed my mind, she and her boyfriend would pay $25 per pill. I said thanks, but no thanks.

She asked me to finish undressing and get on the bed for the massage. She stood directly in front of me, just a few steps away as I took off the last of my clothes and I stood there naked. I felt as if she stood there for me to prove 1 wasn't a cop, who likely would leave at least his underwear on. She pointed to the bed that was now covered in a bright beach towel. I lay face down and she didn't offer anything to cover me up as you would in a traditional massage. She straddled my buttocks and began to massage my back. She told me that she didn't have sex as part of her massage. I assured her that I just wanted a massage from a pretty young lady and I had no other motive. I repeated that I often got massaged from the same older woman and I thought it would be a treat to get a massage from a beautiful young one.

As I lay there, I could see her in the mirror and we talked from this reflection. She pressed the issue of buying the pills. She climbed off of me and stood up next to the bed between me and the mirror. She looked at me as she slowly pulled her sweat pants off exposing a stunning young body and sleek thong underwear. She tugged slightly at her thong to adjust it as she looked over her shoulder in the mirror and checked herself out. She then sat back on top of me while she continued to talk to me, and I watched her in the mirror as she pulled her top off exposing her bare breasts. I kept watching her in the mirror and she was watching me. It got quiet and I needed an ice breaker for the silence, so I quipped that she certainly didn't dress like a cop and she laughed. She bent at the waist as she put her hands to the side of my shoulders and she pressed her bare breasts against my back. She rubbed her breasts on my back and buttocks as she maneuvered her body over mine. I couldn't help but be aroused.

She leaned in close to my ear with her mouth, her young body firmly against my back, and then asked me seductively if I would sell her the Oxy. I told her I would find out how many I had and we could probably work something out and sell them to her. She then asked me to turn over and she sat on me, barely above my crotch. I immediately noticed a tattooed first name of "Steve" on her flat stomach, just right of her belly button. I tapped the tattoo and asked her if that was her boyfriend's name. She leaned into me and whispered, "just some guy who treats me like crap, but I keep going back to him." The fact that she chose to whisper that bit of information convinced me he was outside the open door. As we talked, I described to her that I had a very controlling wife and two young children at home. I told her this because I needed to set some restrictive boundaries; I knew I would need to work within the confines of the narcotics officers, and this would allow me to put her off, buy some time, if I needed it. She talked with me and continued to massage my chest as she straddled my naked body. She reached for my hands and placed them on her young firm breasts. It was an unexpected treat for "an old guy with a script." I'll let you use your imagination from there, but she finished her massage and then we both got dressed. The fish was in the net.

The girl, Ashley, had taken the bait, and I felt confident that I had the deal working. Now I would need to go home and hope my wife's level of understanding would allow me to be completely honest with her about what I was doing, and what I had just done. I knew Lisa wanted to help Brandon and we both knew my involvement would require a venture into unchartered territory, but I needed her to know everything.

Lisa and I had been married for twenty-four years and we knew what lay ahead would be a bigger test of our commitment than what I had just done. We needed to help Brandon and I needed to believe this would also help the kids I was attempting to bust, just as my son getting busted was one step closer to hitting bottom, and hopefully one step closer to getting off of these powerful drugs. There was no turning back now.

Before I got home from my massage, my crack-berry phone rang and it was Ashley. She called me to ask if I could bring her a few Oxys to hold her over for the night. I, of course, didn't have any Oxys, so I told her I couldn't get out and we could do the whole deal at once. I couldn't help but feel sorrow for her and guilt for what I was doing, but I justified it in my mind that she needed to get away from this guy and that she needed to get help for her drug problem as well. I pictured my son and his willingness to do anything to get his next fix.

When I arrived home, I called Officer White and told him I had a drug deal set up with Steve and Ashley and they wanted one hundred Oxy pills. To say he was shocked would be an understatement. He wanted to know how I did this and was I sure it was Steve, as well as numerous other questions. I told him that he had told me he didn't want to know anything, and I preferred to keep it that way for now. I did give Officer White enough information so he was sure I had the right people. I just needed to know when and where the narcotics squad wanted to do this deal and what I needed to do next. The Officer was excited at the opportunity to get this guy and he arranged me coming to the police station so I could make the call to set up the one hundred Oxy pill deal on a recorded phone line. The drug deal itself would happen later, and I would need to be evasive about the where and the when of the actual exchange of money for drugs. I was told to call her from my phone and tell her I would call her tomorrow around noon.

Defining Moments

Chapter 18: Game Time

I arrived at the station and was escorted to an interrogation room. It looked like a carbon copy of the room I was in before but it was further down the hall. Officer White connected a recording device to my crack-berry and I was told to place the call and get Ashley to engage in conversation that would be incriminating. I was to get her to use the word "Oxy" and discuss the price and the quantity and to get Ashley to acknow-ledge that the price was "$2500 cash for the one hundred Oxys." I placed the call, nervous and anxious to be sure to get what the police wanted. To my shock, the recording on Ashley's phone stated it was no longer in service. The officer was obviously disappointed and suggested that perhaps they caught on to the scheme, as they were very savvy. Just as he was rambling on how difficult it was to get someone to deal with you... blah ... blah ... blah, my crack-berry rang. I looked at the caller ID and it was Steve's number, not Ashley's. This was even better since the goal was to get him and she was ancillary. I picked up the phone, which was still connected to the recording device, and she introduced herself and said she was calling from her boyfriend's phone because hers was broken.

The call went better than expected as you could hear Steve coaching her in the background. Ashley fell nicely into all of the comments the police wanted to record. I was told by Officer White to tell her I could meet her in a couple of days as I was out of town. I told her I would call her when I returned and after work hours. She agreed and the call ended. At the time, I didn't understand why we didn't just go do the deal right away, but the cops needed to get a crew together and do all this planning for the bust. Once this part of the deal was confirmed, the officer left the room and returned with a stack of documents for me to sign. I didn't read much of it because it didn't really matter what it said. They were the documents that they needed to cover their asses, period!

Two nervous days passed before I got the go-ahead and a time and location for the drug deal. I was instructed to call Ashley and tell her the time, but not to commit to the location. The police wanted the time to set up the area of the bust location and they did not want the drug dealer to come early and perhaps see them preparing. I was instructed to meet the police over an hour before the scheduled time.

During this entire time since Brandon was busted, my wife and I had been working to detox him. We had him on complete lockdown at the house with no visitors allowed. His room and the entire house were still searched daily, including the CD cases and every nook and cranny. We used the professional drug tests and we tested him randomly. Hopefully he hadn't found a way to get this drug into our home (again). He finished the worst of the drug withdrawals a couple of days after the disastrous intervention.

When Officer White called, the bust was on. I hugged and kissed Brandon and Lisa as if I was about to ship off to a war. I felt guilty that I couldn't say something to my younger son, Bryce, but he was now back at college and we hadn't told him what I was doing for Brandon. I didn't want him to worry and I didn't want him to hate his brother for putting me in this situation. I would tell him later when all was well... hopefully. If not, I needed to tell my wife to tell him how much I loved him, just in case. She broke down and I left the house before she had recomposed herself.

I received my first instructions at the police station. Told to follow two undercover cars to the back of a nearby hotel, we were met by about a dozen different police officers in varying attire. Some were in marked squad cars, but most looked like everything from an ordinary guy to a punk with a beanie on his head. Scruffy beards to cleanly shaven, they were an unlikely melting pot of law enforcement. They were driving a variety of cars and trucks, old and new. It was beginning to get dark and that is what the officers wanted. I was instructed by Officer White to stand beside my truck while two officers searched the vehicle and verified that I had no weapon, cash or drugs inside. Then I was searched and the officers asked me to remove my shirt so they could wire me up. I stood there arms out in this parking lot surrounded by police, as they taped this wire to my body. Several cars drove slowly through the hotel parking lot, gawking. I stared back at them trying not to look ashamed, hoping one of my neighbors or clients didn't drive by. It must have looked like I was getting arrested!

I could hear the police and undercover officers talking about me amongst themselves. In one exchange, a uniform officer asked an undercover officer what they busted me for and who I was turning on. The undercover officer told him I was the father of a kid they busted and I was "working my son's deal." The uniform officer responded that he had never heard of that before, to which the undercover officer replied that this, as far as he knew, was a first.

After I was wired, tested, and instructed to put my shirt and jacket back on, the briefing began. A loose circle of about a dozen officers stood between my truck and the van that would record the sting from the wire I was wearing. I would call the target soon and instruct her to meet me in a particular spot. Things moved rapidly now and the instructions came quickly. I was instructed to get as much incriminating conversation as I could, including the price, quantity and name of the drug; anything beyond that would be helpful, but gravy. The main thing was to get the money for the drugs.

Then I was shown the contents of a small white plastic bottle: One hundred Oxys poured into the officer's hand. They were smaller than I thought they would be and an odd green color. He gathered the pills back into the bottle and handed them to me, telling me to put them in an easily accessible jacket pocket.

The officers were all gathered around, but my focus was now entirely on the lead man, Officer White, the same undercover officer who had busted my son, had screwed up by giving Brandon the wrong phone number and with whom I had negotiated this deal. He was cocky and his ego always front and center, but I completely understood this demeanor. A person who does this for a living should have a high level of confidence, and that translates into what one might call "a strong personality."

I was listening as if my life depended on these men. It did. I was told that I would also be arrested in a mock arrest so that the dealers would think we were all busted. I would be handcuffed against the truck or on the ground and led to a separate patrol car. Oh boy, the handcuffs I had successfully avoided most of my life were finally finding their way on my wrists.

"After you have the cash and they have the pills, tell 'em you're going to head to Tahoe. That will be our signal."

I could handle that.

Defining Moments

When I was given the shots fired and weapon instructions, I realized that desperate druggies rob guys like me. The officer began to explain what I was to do if this turned out to be a robbery. Apparently, this Steve was known to carry a weapon and he was known to come up a little short on cash for drug deals and if the seller wasn't willing to accept the lower amount, he might brandish his weapon. If he pulled the gun or a weapon of any sort, the officers needed me to indicate that.

"How about 'gun, gun, he's got a fucking gun'"? I asked.

"How about, 'there's no need for guns,'" the officer countered. This was an unexpected instruction and a situation I hadn't realistically contemplated.

I was all wired up and the officer flattened his hand out and tapped on my truck's windowsill to illustrate how low they wanted me.

"You get here in the crossfire." He bent me down behind my driver's side door. "You stay here. No moving around."

He told me that in the case of a weapon, they would come in from both sides of the truck with their guns drawn. The shooting officers would be on the driver's side firing over my head. (How comforting). What had I gotten myself into? I didn't want brains splattered all over my truck, especially if they were mine!

I was then shown pictures so I could verify Ashley and recognize Steve. It was her, and his head was practically shaved bald. He looked like your typical punk kid, just like Brandon.

"Is his hair still that short?" I asked.

"Not the last I saw. Why?"

"Well, if his hair is longer, I can at least grab him by the head if he pulls a gun on me."

At this point I was given a lecture and the shots fired instructions again, because apparently I hadn't gotten the message the first time.

I was to stay in my truck and tell them to get in when they arrived. I was also told that the dealers would try to move me to another location and I was to stand my ground and never agree to move, even if it was just across the street. Steve had a warrant for his arrest in this county so he would attempt to avoid it. The officers would be placed all around me and my movement would ruin the bust and endanger me and the officers. I guess only time would tell how things would go down and we prepared to head to

76

Wal-Mart parking lot for the big bust. I personally would rather be shot at Nordstrom's!

Once in place at the store, I was contacted via my regular cell phone and I was told to make the call to Ashley and tell her where I would meet her in twenty minutes. The marked police cars were out of site and honestly, I couldn't see one officer, undercover or otherwise. The unmarked cars were apparently mixed into the parking lot full of cars. I made the call and Ashley answered quickly. I told her where I would be in twenty minutes, which was exactly where I was already. She immediately tried to get me to meet her at the apartment where she massaged me. I told her I had a brief window of time and I needed to pick up some items for my wife at the store so that was the only place and the only way I could meet them. She agreed and said she would see me soon. After I hung up the phone, the officer called me on my personal cell phone, which I was answering from a headset in my ear. He offered some encouraging words about how I had handled her attempt to move me and said they would try to move me again because Steve was not going to want to meet me in this county because of his arrangement with the police here. We were only a mile from another county line, so Officer White and his team felt he would try to get me to move that mile. I hung up and the wait began.

I was all eyes and all ears as the silence in the truck made it too easy for my mind to wander. I wasn't allowed any background noise. I was parked at the far end of the lot with the front end of my truck against a fence as I was instructed to do. I was impatiently waiting when I finally saw one of the scraggly dressed officers wander by pushing a grocery basket full of bags looking like a homeless person. He had an old torn jacket on with a beanie on his head. He was unshaven and looked the part of a vagrant. We had a moment of eye contact and he had no expression as if he didn't know me at all. It was a slight reassurance, but I still wondered where the rest of them were and how they would get to me quick if things went to Hell. I received another call from the officer and he had me speak so they could tune in the wire. He said that they needed to occasionally check the wire—from time to time I should say something to reassure them that they'd end up with a quality recording of the deal.

Defining Moments

The crack-berry rang and it was Ashley. She said her friend was reluctant to come to where I was because I was in a county where they were tough on crime and she wanted me to drive a couple of miles away and meet them at a grocery store. I told her again that I didn't have much time and it was already past twenty minutes. The deal would happen where I was or it wouldn't happen, period! I told her to get her shit together or I was leaving. I was short, irritated and aggressive as an act to get them to come to me. Ashley said she would talk to her boyfriend and call me right back.

Another call from the officer telling me I was doing fine and to hang in there and hold my position. A call from Ashley followed and she stated that her boyfriend was unwilling to come to me so either I meet them at their chosen destination or the deal was off. I told her to forget the deal and I would sell the drugs through my friend who I mentioned during the massage if she couldn't get the boyfriend calmed down.

Ashley said she would work on him but that tonight was off. As I hung up, I was crushed that this was not happening! All of this prep, stress, planning and nothing to show for it! My mind filled with thoughts of my son going to prison with my inability to deliver Steve to the narcotics officers to satisfy Brandon's deal with them.

The call from the officer came in on my headset and it was to the point; I was instructed to head back to the spot where I was wired—"home-base"—so I began my short journey back, completely disappointed. The entourage of police came out of parking spots and the marked cars came from behind the building and out of nowhere. It was as if a sudden parade had emerged from nowhere, folding in behind me as I exited the parking lot. I arrived at the original briefing spot and I got out of the truck and the lead officer immediately began to tell me this was a good first contact and that I would get them. I tried to interrupt him with my feelings of distress but he would have no part of it. He complimented me on holding my ground so firmly. In fact, he and his partner asked me if I had done this before because I was so stern with her and refused to bend. I guess they were accustomed to dealing with strung out drug addicts. I was still completely disappointed and I told them so. I just wanted this over and I had every expectation that it would be finished tonight and I could get on with my life and my son could get on with rehab and hopefully get healthy.

Once I was un-wired I was able to call my wife who was a sobbing mess. Not hearing from me and the uncertainty of the night had taken its toll on her and my son. I headed home defeated and unsure if I would ever get the opportunity to complete the task that would free my son from a three to five year prison term. I was mentally exhausted and I didn't know what my next move would be. All I knew was that the officers told me that if Ashley contacted me, I was to put her off until next week because they couldn't put a crew together until the following Tuesday. Not only did I need to put humpty dumpty (the drug deal) back together again, I had to do it on a specific day at a specific time and in a county that the dealers clearly didn't want anything to do with. It seemed to be an impossible set of circumstances which would need to simultaneously occur to accomplish my task, and oh yeah, I needed to do it without getting shot.

Defining Moments

Chapter 19: A Second Chance

A couple of days passed before the crack-berry rang in my car. The ring tone surprised me, as it was a sound I wasn't accustomed to hearing. At first I thought it was a sound on the car radio but quickly realized it must be Ashley. She was obviously the only person who had this number and she was very apologetic for the failure to show. Ashley said she wanted to get the Oxys as soon as possible and that there would be no problems this time, as she knew Steve was completely out of product and would meet me on my terms. In a judgment call that I had not previously planned, I flatly told her that I already sold the Oxys through the other buyer that I had told her about. She was notably upset and actually confronted me on my "promise" to sell them to her. I pointed out that I waited in a parking lot for her for over an hour and she was the one who flaked. I described how easy it was to sell the one hundred Oxys to the other guy and that he met me exactly where I wanted and when I wanted, gave me the cash and it was a breeze! She asked me if I had any more and I told her I had a few but not enough to trouble with. I then told her that I had a refill available for ninety Oxys that was good to fill next Tuesday. I swear I was making this dialogue up as I went along, just to fit all the necessary criteria and to put her off until next Tuesday. The new prescription combined with what I already had would meet the quantity of one hundred Oxys that they wanted. I also wanted a solid clarification that I was only going to meet on my terms, just as I had in my fictitious deal. Did I mention I am in sales? Telling her I sold the drugs to someone else is the classic "take-away" which creates an urgency and desire to comply. She said they would buy the Oxys and they would meet me where I wanted. She assured me that there would be no bullshit this time. I told her I would call her and give her the meeting place after I filled the prescription.

I called the lead narcotics officer and informed him of my conversation. Again he was amazed at my creativity with the concoction of the take away story. I told him why I did it that way and that I only wanted to wear a wire one more time. He said to call him to confirm the timing.

Defining Moments

A call to the officer confirmed we were on for 6 p.m. that night. I was instructed to call Ashley around 6 p.m. and tell her I would meet her as soon as I could get out of the house, and that I would call her when I left it. I prepared myself emotionally for another unpredictable evening. I was told to meet the officers at a different location behind a nearby grocery store near the loading dock and trash bins. I arrived promptly, eager to get this thing done, and was immediately disappointed to learn that there would be a delay getting the crew together as they had just busted an Ecstasy dealer and part of the crew was stuck hauling, booking and questioning him. I was irritated as they wired me up in anticipation of the bust. The officers then recorded my call to Ashley where I told her my wife had me watching the kids and unavailable until she returned, so I'd call her in a while. I was buying an unknown amount of time while keeping Ashley and Steve on the hook.

So while I am standing in the lot wired up, not able to call my wife, not able to go anyplace myself, some of the officers take orders for a hamburger run! I am now beyond irritated, as their lackadaisical attitude could equal another disappointment and a setback for the mission to get my son on with his life and out of a possible prison sentence. They asked me what I wanted from the nearby hamburger joint as they relayed orders to another officer via a cell phone. I wanted nothing! Eating was the last thing on my mind and my stomach was churning with every passing moment. I just wanted to get on with it and go home in one piece. It was an odd sight for me as I watched these officers chow down their burgers and sip on their drinks, reminiscing about the drug deal they just finished. Just another day at the office, I guess.

A moment later, my crack-berry starts to blow up with one call after the next from Ashley, wanting to know when we are doing this deal. I must keep buying time with excuses, now nearing a two-hour delay waiting for the cops to come from the other bust. It is looking like this deal is not going to happen either. I answer some of the calls and ignore others as I am instructed to do by Officer White. I whisper during one call as if I can't talk because I am still stuck at home with my wife and cannot talk freely. I reassure Ashley that I will meet her as soon as I can get out. I think of my wife and son at home wondering why I haven't called; is it over? Am I dead?

Finally the crew is all present behind the store and the review of protocol and procedure began as it did before. New officers are in amongst familiar faces from the prior attempt. I find myself less interested in their chat as I mentally prepare myself for the task at hand. I am given the weapons and shots fired instructions again. In my usual humorous deflection of discomfort, I quip that the last time I met Ashley it was a "happy ending" and I would like the same result this time. The officers are un-amused.

The officers are sent to stake out a nearby drugstore. My story to the drug dealers will be that I will fill the prescription there and meet her in that parking lot as it is a stone's throw within the county line which they want the bust in. One problem I point out is that the drugstore will be closed in a few minutes, but they send the crew that direction for feedback on the location. The call comes back that the parking lot is virtually empty of cars, leaving no cover for the officers. I am starting to feel like I know more about this drug busting business than the cops.

After a change of venue to a nearby grocery store down the street and several miles within the county line, it is nearly 9 p.m. and I have been unable to call my wife for over three hours. The officers move into place for the bust. Several marked police cars hide in an adjacent apartment complex that has a driveway into the grocery store parking lot at the opposite end of the shopping center. I am instructed to park my truck's front end against a fence that borders the parking lot facing the greenbelt. I am shown new surveillance photos of the two suspects and their vehicle: a red Dodge Charger with tinted windows. The code word which I am to use in a sentence to confirm the exchange of money for drugs has been changed to "Reno" and I see a pattern so I assume that if the deal does not go down this time, my next code word may be "Vegas." I pray there isn't a next time.

Defining Moments

Chapter 20: Going Down

Finally, a red Dodge Charger is driving slowly over the entrance bridge. I say, "Red Dodge Charger approaching at one o'clock," attempting not to move my lips, as the vehicle is coming almost directly towards me on my right. The Dodge slows almost to a stop just a couple of car lengths away. I am unable to see in the tinted windows of the car, but I am certain they can see me; I stare back as if to say, "Is that you?" They are obviously aware that I am there, alone and awaiting their arrival. The car slowly pulls away after taking a good look at me. I lose sight of them, as they seem to be going towards the opposite end of the parking lot. I assume they will pull around after checking out the surroundings, but instead my crack-berry rings within seconds. It is Ashley and she is trying to move me to a Starbucks that is on the other side of the same parking lot.

I resist and ask her if that was her that stopped next to me in the red Dodge Charger. She says it was, but she would rather meet at the Starbucks where there are some people around. I tell her to just come to my truck and let's get this deal done. Ashley states she is suspicious that I won't drive a hundred yards to meet her. I make a judgment call that I know will not make the undercover narcotics team happy, but she is right. What is my great reason justifying not driving a short distance? I tell her I will drive right over and park by the Starbucks.

I hang up with her and I state into my wire that we are moving to the Starbucks and to deal with it. My head set rings from my personal cell phone and the lead officer is a combination of irritated and understanding but he warns me to drive slowly and not to get too far in front of the van which will be coming in behind me. I am already backing up as he speaks to me. I am told to park against something, a wall or a spot in front of a store but not to park in the middle of the lot leaving all sides open. I notice the surveillance van coming up one of the aisles as I pull onto the same path the Dodge Charger took, which leads directly to the Starbucks. The van pulls in behind me at a comfortable distance. I am headed towards the other end of the parking lot where I know the apartment complex is hiding the marked police cars. I move slowly towards the coffee shop and my heart is beating out of my chest.

So many thoughts are running through my head and I can't seem to clear them. After the millions of thoughts and moments that have haunted me during this evening I begin to focus on my current life, not my past. I think of my wife who has been left in silence for nearly four hours. I think of my sons, Brandon, completely fucked up from his drug addiction and Bryce, away at college completely unaware of what is happening and what risk his dad is about to take. It occurs to me that Bryce and my wife may never forgive Brandon if something were to happen to me.

I recall their little league baseball games and soccer teams I coached. All of the art projects which we proudly displayed with the help of refrigerator magnets over the years. Particular events in their life pop in and out of my head. Their future begins to enter my mind and I hope and pray that I will see Brandon free from his addiction one day and see Bryce graduate college. Who will they marry one day? How many children will they have? Will I be a grandpa or a memory? Perhaps all this worrying is for nothing or perhaps the worst is about to happen. I must cleanse my mind of this sudden bombardment of thoughts and I must focus!

I pull into the parking lot of the Starbucks just as my crack-berry rings. I see Ashley standing inside the coffee shop with her cell phone up to her ear. I answer the phone as I notice a space directly facing the front door of Starbucks is opening up as a car begins to back out. She asks me where I am and I tell her I am looking at her from in the truck waiting for that front spot to open. She sees me, and as we talk I can see her lips move slightly ahead of the sound of her voice. I didn't see the red Dodge Charger anywhere when I was pulling in, and I don't see it now. I scan the people around Ashley as I am pulling forward, but Steve, the young man in the surveillance photo, the boyfriend and drug dealer, is nowhere to be seen. What I can't see worries me more than what I can see, as I scan my surroundings. Ashley continues to talk as I look directly at her. She says she will get in the car when I park and I watch her hang up the phone as she walks towards the door I am now facing. As Ashley reaches for the door, she brings her phone up to her ear as if she has an incoming call. She is close enough for me to read her lips, just in front of the truck, her hand pushing the door open. "Fuck" is the only word she mouths as her eyes make contact with mine; she is immediately in a panic. She looks wildly at me as she turns and runs back into the Starbucks, frantically making her way through the patrons headed towards the back of the shop.

I have no idea what just happened. I sit there dumbfounded, thinking the worst and that we have lost this bust forever. Maybe she saw something or the phone call was from her boyfriend who had seen something. I call her on her cell phone and to my surprise she answers. She is frantic. She quickly states that they left, the deal is off and they are headed home. Her voice echoes as if she is in a closet. I know she hasn't left because I just saw her run to the back of a Starbucks that I know well. She is nearly in tears and suddenly hangs up. I call the officer from my blue-tooth not knowing what is happening or what to do. I know they can hear me through the wire, but I cannot hear them. Officer White tells me they have the male in custody as he was hiding the car in the apartment complex and he ran right into all of the marked police cars and attempted to run. The cops blocked him off with some unmarked cars that had been on him since his Dodge had slowed next to my truck. He tells me they are looking for the girl and ask me if I know anything about her whereabouts. I tell him where I last saw her and I add that her last call had an echo sound. I tell him that the back of that Starbucks is the bathroom so perhaps she is hiding in it.

Other officers in the van hear my message as it is broadcast over my wire. They quickly get the information out and officers both under-cover and uniformed come out of the woodworks and rush around me towards the Starbucks. Officer White firmly tells me to "return to home-base now." The officer's phone hangs up suddenly. I put the truck in reverse and begin to back out amongst the mayhem. I notice all of the patrons headed in different directions as the police are yelling for everyone to get down. I feel as though I am watching a movie on a screen. I don't even feel like I am a part of it. As I begin to pull away, more officers are headed in. I look through the Starbucks' window as I put the car in drive to leave and I can see the commotion in the back as the officers' drag Ashley out of the bathroom area and toss her to the floor. I am gone.

Defining Moments

I drive to "home base" (behind the grocery store) where all this started so many hours ago. I am safe but I still can't call my wife because I am wired and those were part of my many instructions. I wait silently by myself wondering if this bust will count for my son or whether there was even a bust at all. Over thirty minutes of silence passes and Officer White pulls up and I ready myself because I now have a million questions. As he gets out of his car, I begin to blurt out my questions and he tells me he must disconnect the wire before we can talk. I reach for my waist and pull the wire off before he can help me. I hold it out to him, he takes it from me and turns it off, and he says, "We got them." I am so relieved, but that is only one answer to one question and I have many.

The deal was done. It was over. I then called my wife who was so wound up from the lack of communication over such a long period of time. She sobbed uncontrollably as I told her I was unharmed, headed home, the ordeal was over and we busted the drug dealers. A hero's welcome awaited me, as my son was so thankful for what I had done for him. As I went to bed that night, my mind would not shut off and the events of that evening replayed in my head over and over again. I lay awake for hours wondering what would have happened if the dealer hadn't run into the cops. They both confessed to the drug deal when separately interrogated. The officer said they had less than half of the money, which she had attempted to hide in a trash can in the Starbucks' bathroom, and Steve had a gun, which Ashley admitted they would have used if I didn't give them the drugs once I discovered they were short on cash. They were going to rob me at gunpoint!

I had literally dodged a bullet.

Part II: After the Bust
Chapter 21: When You Least Expect It

The next morning I woke up before my wife and son. After I brewed my morning coffee, I walked down the hall and back into my bedroom where I kept the drug test in my closet. I walked into Brandon's room and told him to wake up and urinate in the test cup. It was still early and he begged me to let him sleep a little longer, saying he hadn't slept well. I insisted, and told him he could lie back down after the test. Since I knew he had a device called a Wizinator that is sold at smoke shops to look like you are pissing—it has a bag filled with either synthetic urine or someone else's—I made him show me he was really pissing. After he complied, he crawled back into bed. Positive for Oxy. Top of the scale positive.

I looked over at Brandon to see him peering at me from the bed, knowing that drug tests don't lie but drug addicts do. I screamed at him to pack his shit and get the fuck out. I had been left with only one option—to toss Brandon out on the street to hit bottom—because what I was doing wasn't enough.

Or maybe what I was doing was too much?

I had just risked my life to help him and apparently while I was getting wired to save his ass, he had managed to get Oxy into my home and got high while I was working his undercover drug deal. Not only was I devastated, I was a sucker and a fool to have helped him.

After all of the agony during detox, he was back on this shit and nothing had changed.

My love for him and our effort and commitment to him as his parents weren't as strong as his desire to ingest Oxy. Brandon's addiction to this drug was more powerful than anything I could offer and all the love Lisa and I could show.

My wife woke to my screaming and she was as shocked as I was when I showed her the test results. Brandon had to want to get better. As he packed his meager belongings, I grabbed the hand held video player and replayed the footage I had taped of him detoxing. He begged me to stop the video as he could hear himself on it screaming in agony as his body craved this drug. Brandon was crying uncontrollably as he tried to look away from the video that I continued to shove in front of his face. Lisa stood there pale and exhausted, frightened like the night of his intervention. As I remember it, she resembled my mother, so many years before, when we visited Thomas in prison. Lisa could not add even a word.

Brandon left our home with little in his hands and got into what was once a nice little car, but was now something appropriate for a salvage yard with body damage, a driver's door that wouldn't open, and water leaking through missing door seals. Brandon had to get in from the passenger side of this wreck of a car, symbolic of his wreck of a life.

My wife and I held each other as we watched him back out of the driveway. He couldn't even look at us as he drove away to God knows where. We were numb. Our son was 6'2" about 135 pounds and addicted to one of the most powerful drugs on the street: Oxycontin. What would happen to him? Would he get busted again, overdose or die in a drug deal gone bad? We contemplated the worst as we watched what was our son, our first-born, drive off into complete uncertainty. We didn't know Brandon at all, and we really believed we might never see him again. On the day of his birth which seemed like yesterday, I had watched as his little body took its first breath and now I felt like I might be watching him take his last.

We chose not to tell any of my wife's family because we were quite frankly, embarrassed. My wife's family was similar to the 1950s TV Cleavers, and we didn't think they would understand, so for now it remained a family secret. I selfishly didn't want their advice or opinions because I didn't expect them to ever understand. In their defense, they grew up in such a pure family environment that they were ill prepared for the drama that surrounded my upbringing. I have come to understand their view of me as a shady character, and the unlikely marriage of my kind to their perfect daughter, and I have accepted the fact that my past was a freak show compared to their lives. Now I had a contemporary freak-drama in my home, and didn't think they'd be much help with it.

My family on the other hand, was pre-disastered. I hadn't talked to Thomas in several years, except for a few holidays where my mother made it difficult for me not to. Despite getting married and having children, Thomas never settled down. He had been in and out of rehab for decades. Thomas had become very volatile and was making financial demands of us in order to see his children, our nieces and nephews, the boys' cousins. His behavior was erratic and unpredictable. I just didn't understand why he kept repeating the same destructive behavior. Now I had the same question regarding my son. I couldn't help either of them. I had pretty much given up on Thomas, and I was afraid to give up on Brandon.

Over the years, Thomas had conned me out of thousands of dollars. He had an uncanny ability to put together some huge deal making himself absurd amounts of money and then blowing it all on a high roller lifestyle, followed by being completely broke and desperate and addicted to drugs again and again. Thomas had also conned or borrowed thousands of dollars from mutual friends and associates and it was not uncommon for my wife and me to be confronted by angry people in restaurants or public places because my brother owed them money. The last straw with Thomas was over Christmas many years back when he became so violent and threatening that Lisa and I decided to not see him or his family again. We even told our children that if Uncle Thomas came to our house or ever tried to get them in a car that they were to run to any other adult. We did not know what drug he was on or how far he would go.

When he moved to southern California, we were not faced with Thomas's problems anymore. I crossed him off of my list—the brother who had stood shoulder to shoulder with me through all the moves, the abuse, and so much else. The brother, who for a while was all I had, was completely estranged from me. I had put Thomas in a similar category as my biological father, Richard. I considered that in both of their cases, nothing good seemed to happen when I associated with them, so I just kept them out of my life and my family's as well.

The latest stories I had heard about Thomas were that while he had escalated his abuse to injecting heroin, he then attended a drug rehab center called Narconon, which had apparently enabled him to be clean for the last couple of years. If this was true, and he was clean, maybe he'd be a good person to go to for help? My mother thought so, and she insisted that we reach out to him. We were obviously reluctant and for good reason, but we were also desperate.

My mother insisted that Thomas's last rehab stint at Narconon had worked for Thomas and she knew he had strong ties there and perhaps he could get Brandon in for treatment. She told us that Thomas was doing work for the rehab in the form of interventions and getting drug addicts into treatment and that was what Brandon needed. But at what price? I wasn't as worried about the financial price at this point, but rather the thought of owing Thomas after all that he had perpetrated against us was almost as unpalatable as Brandon's Oxy addiction. This was all unchartered territory. It was all uncomfortable. It all sucked big time.

My pride would take a back seat to Brandon's needs. His drug problem was more important than the grudge I was holding over my brother's drug-induced antics. I felt like I was selling out. But somewhere in my heart I guess I had always hoped that Thomas and I would mend the damage between us. That one day I could forgive. That one day our families would spend a holiday together, and that holiday would lead to another and eventually things would be as normal as they could be.

Part of me also felt that my older brother was in need of a way to get back in good graces of the family and that maybe I could give this to him by reaching out.

I contacted Thomas in desperation, and he did have the connections to get my son into Narconon, a private rehab program that we couldn't afford.

We put the word out through some of Brandon's friends that his Uncle Thomas could help him get into this private rehab if he wanted the help, but Brandon had to want it.

Chapter 22: In Sight of the Bottom

About a month had passed since we talked with Thomas and sent the word out to Brandon. Last we heard, Brandon was about 400 miles south working with a friend. I wondered what prison would be like for Brandon, and wished he were in prison because at least we'd know where he was; he wouldn't be a drug addict wandering the streets. Strange irony, that. Strange feeling it stirred in me, realizing that my intervention to keep Brandon out of prison could backfire so terribly. Before he got help now, he would need to hit rock bottom. Hopefully he'd survive it.

Then, one day Thomas called. Brandon just contacted him from some street corner in a bad part of town outside of San Diego. Brandon said he was broke, addicted, alone and ready to commit himself to rehab. Thomas said he had dropped what he was doing and was driving directly to find him, as he knew Brandon might change his mind. Thomas said that most drug addicts would take every drug they could get their hands on if they knew they were going to rehab, and this was dangerous. He was off to the rescue! Thomas called again when he had Brandon in his car, saying while Brandon looked horrible, he was alive and on his way to a detox center, which would be followed by rehab—hopefully. My brother had connections at this rehab center. It's a big one, called Narconon, a non-profit operated by the Church of Scientology, to which my brother belongs. We are not Scientologists, but honestly I didn't care who was running the program. I had heard my fair share of opinions and criticism of this religion, but it just didn't outweigh the other options.

"Honestly," I told Lisa, "I don't care if he comes out with a shaved head and a pony tail selling incense at the airport, as long as he comes out clean and sober with the ability to deal with his addiction."

She agreed.

As we put one foot in front of the other, his journey would begin, hour-by-hour, followed by a day, then a week, and hopefully he would embrace the program and discover whatever was causing his self-destructive behavior. Early on, I had many phone calls and up-dates from the staff of the rehab center as to

Brandon's progress, some good and most bad. He craved this drug and he would say anything to get it. He would claim he was in extreme pain and he needed a doctor or anything as an excuse to escape to the outside world.

These counselors had heard it all before; as former drug addicts they had used the same tactics. He was an adult and could leave the rehab center anytime he wanted, but the staff was well trained in convincing him otherwise. Everyone I talked to at Narconon had been through the program themselves and were former addicts. The young man assigned to our son was wonderful. He explained that he had been through over a dozen programs before this program resolved his cravings and addressed his issues. He had been clean for six years, and I could only pray for the same result. He had worked there since he graduated the program and he assured me they would do their best to help Brandon.

The facility where Brandon was staying was nearly a nine-hour drive from our home. We talked to Brandon on the phone occasionally and every time we did it was as if a cloud was slowly lifting and he was starting to think more clearly. He seemed to be growing up. He had never really matured like his younger brother because in his world of drugs he was not living reality. Easter was rolling around and we planned on visiting him with the family, but only if he completed certain parts of his program by Easter. If so, he would be allowed a LOA (Leave Of Absence) for the day. If not, we would have Easter with him at the facility. He would have been an inpatient for over two months by then and the Narconon program would keep him as long as they needed until he was ready to graduate or until he left on his own. We could only hope that Brandon stayed with the program and left only when he had the tools to stay off the dope.

In the meantime, I handled the balance of Brandon's court appointments with a power of attorney and I dealt personally with Officer White to have his charges dropped. I appeared in court for Brandon in an environment I wouldn't wish on my worst enemy. Young and old alike were escorted into the courtroom, shackled at the hands and ankles in their jail issued orange jump suits. They shuffled their feet along the ground as they entered the room. They looked defeated and unhealthy as the officers who escorted them cuffed each one to a chain that ran beneath the benches as they awaited their hearings or sentencing.

I imagined my son in their place. I wished my son was there to see what could have been. The audience in the courtroom was a colorful mixture of society's misfits and their families. Again I found myself hoping nobody would recognize me or my son's name plastered for all to see on the hearings notice sheet attached to the courtroom door. These fatherly duties seemed minimal after what I had already done and I was happy to do this because he was getting the help he needed. I was still humiliated to be there and to see my last name on the court docket clipboard.

Easter weekend, Lisa, Bryce and I drove over eight hours towards Temecula, California, then over a rural road through a desert valley to Werner Springs. There was no mistaking our destination when we spotted it. It looked like the recreation yard in the film *One Flew Over the Coo Coo's Nest*, as people milled about, stopping and turning to look at us as we entered the parking lot. The facility itself might have been a roadside migrant worker motel. People were roaming around the grounds doing everything from raking leaves to just hanging in groups, but each one stopped what they were doing to examine us as we drove in. We could immediately tell that visitors to this desolate location were rare.

Brandon approached the vehicle with enthusiasm and the brightest, broadest smile we had ever seen on his face. We instantly noticed his weight gain and he proudly announced through our open car window that he was nearing 170 pounds, and he looked healthy for the first time in so many years. His complexion was clear and his eyes were the bright blue they once were and the whites of his eyes were shiny and clear. Brandon could hardly wait for us to open the car door, and he embraced each of us as if he hadn't seen us in years. I know I hadn't seen him like this in years. He held me so tightly and so long. He hadn't hugged me like that since he was a young child.

Our son shared a twelve-by-twelve-foot room and one bathroom with three people. One of his roommates was my age. This was no celebrity rehab for sure. It did have a nice pool area and a sauna, which they used in a detoxification program designed to rid the body of drugs and residue, Brandon explained. The pool area was the highlight of the facility, but the staff was warm and friendly. I noticed a bus parked out front, slowly loading with students and staff. I asked a staffer where they were going, and was surprised when he told me they were headed to a Catholic church for Easter services. I told him I thought this was a Scientology-based program, to which he replied that, while this was a common misconception, they did not favor or push any religion. A shame, he stated, as this keeps some people away from a very good rehabilitation center where everyone is allowed to practice whatever religion they wish. My wife and I had attended Alanon meetings back home, and we found them very religious in structure, so we expected some Scientology leanings out here in the desert, but found no evidence of any.

Our son proudly toured us around the grounds and introduced us to everyone we passed. He was so enthusiastic and so different. Although he was excited to see us, he was calm and collected. He was respectful to all and excited to show off his family. He seemed to know everyone. We met many of the people who we spoke with on the phone and got to put their faces with their names. Every worker we met was a recovering drug addict and a one-time student of Narconon. People from all walks of life, from all over the country and all ages; it was a mosaic of America's addicts trying to change their lives. The longer the students were there, the more naturally they mentored the new arrivals. After about a half hour visiting the center, the facility had transformed for us—from a roadside dive motel to an oasis of healing.

We took Brandon out to Thomas's for Easter brunch, about an hour away. In that hour, a young man, our son, was in our vehicle and he spoke with confidence and newfound wisdom about what he was learning and how he was being taught to apply it to real life situations. At the brunch, the family watched as this same young man who was the subject of an intervention just a few months earlier, spoke calmly, listened to others and acted like a normal human being. We could not ignore this massive transformation in just two months as an inpatient. Lisa and I were thrilled. Giddy even.

We drove Brandon back to the facility where they immediately drug tested him. It was routine, and he knew to expect it. We were allowed to stay until 8 p.m. and he was not about to let us leave one minute early. Brandon had been isolated so long; he just wanted to be with us, just to sit on a bench and talk. Before we left I told him that very few people in this world could say they were in the best place in the world they could be and that was exactly where he was. I told him that the irony was that the second best place in the world for him would have been prison. He agreed. As we prepared to leave we were treated with the same long embrace as when we arrived. As we drove off down the narrow road, Brandon waved.

Could we really be getting our son back? We knew at least for now, he was exactly where he should be. He was far from the streets he once roamed and free from the drugs he once craved.

Defining Moments

Chapter 23: The Where, When & Why of Drugs

We talked to Brandon as often as he could and we kept in touch with the counselors weekly. Over the next two months we received calls from our son and his counselor as he was in the part of the program where he was assigned to come clean with his family, acknowledge his behavior, and confess to the many terrible things he had done. The calls were very hard on us because even though they were necessary, we felt like he was getting so much better and we were getting all this bad news about stuff in the past. We understood that this was a necessary part of his treatment; he needed to cleanse himself and ask for our forgiveness. At the end of every confession he would ask if we would accept him back into the family to which we always answered yes! Every time Brandon called he seemed more mentally clear.

Brandon's counseling had revealed several things that had caused him to bury himself in drugs and he was learning how to manage those painful experiences. One big event was when our son received a call from another friend of his while we were away on a family vacation. The friend told Brandon that his best friend, Tom, had been in a horrible car accident and was near death. Our son, like Tom, just sixteen years old, was hysterical, and we returned home immediately. It seemed like half of the high school was holding a vigil at the hospital when we arrived. Tom was paralyzed from the waist down in the accident.

Car washes were held as fundraisers for this handsome and popular young man whose family had no health insurance. Tom was always such a bright spot and had an infectious personality. As time went on, Brandon never stopped being his best friend. At sixteen years old Brandon was helping his young friend with everything from carrying him into a car or up the stairs, to helping him on the toilet or into a bath. They would race down our hallway in the wheelchair laughing and carrying on like nothing was amiss.

Often Tom's father invited Brandon over to help his son through his darker depressed moments and we would always allow it, no matter what time of the day or night. I was so impressed by Brandon's mature behavior and his unwavering friendship and love for Tom.

One day Tom's father called me to thank me for Brandon's friendship to his son. He was emotional when he called as he told me that long after the fundraisers, gatherings and phone calls for his son had stopped, only one friend was still calling and visiting and it was Brandon. I was so very proud of him.

One evening, less than a year later, Brandon cancelled a night out with his friends, including Tom. He didn't feel like going out. His wheelchair-bound friend went anyway. The phone rang late that night with the unbelievable news of another car accident. This time Tom's paralyzed body was thrown through the window and he tumbled down the highway to his death. Brandon was inconsolable. His best friend was dead. Brandon blamed himself for not being there to take care of Tom. One of Brandon's confessions during rehab was that almost all of his friends decided to get as high as they could to attend Tom's funeral. It was the beginning of his excessive drug abuse.

Chapter 24: Let The Healing Begin

As Brandon approached his fifth month as a student at Narconon, he called us and told us he was nearing graduation from the program. He also told us he had applied for an internship at the facility and that he wanted to become a drug counselor. Brandon told us he wanted to give back and stay on to help others and told us how much better equipped he felt to deal with the world which surrounds us all, but silently haunts a select few. The counselors at Narconon had such a profound impact on him that he wanted to have the same impact on others. We felt as though we were getting our son back!

We made the long drive to attend the graduation ceremony with our younger son, Bryce, my mother, my in-laws—who were no longer in the dark—and my brothers. It was a gathering including all the students and the staff. Prior to the ceremony we were invited to eat dinner with everyone. We walked the food line with all who attended. A variety of foods were spooned into our plates and it was chow time in the mess hall. We were seated close to the front in a crowded cafeteria room. The room was a scattering of mismatched tables and chairs and old couches that were obviously a collection of donations. It started with accolades and awards for those early in their treatment and worked its way through the students by their personal achievements inching towards the finale of the three students set to "graduate" tonight. Everyone who was recognized for reaching a new level of their treatment was welcome to speak if they wished. Those who were in the program longer were more likely to do so, thanking others (both students and staff) for helping them through their most difficult challenges. Some were very emotional and some were humorous. All were heartfelt and meaningful descriptions of their individual challenges to reach that next level. It was clear that everyone here, whether they were staff or student, had the ability to impact anyone they touched.

When the moment arrived for this evening's three graduates to speak, a young lady in her early twenties walked to the front of the room with her head down. When she looked up, she smiled nervously. She had no family present. She told everyone how her mother told her how ugly she was her whole life and told her she was worthless, how she attempted to numb the pain with the drugs she took. How she became addicted to the drugs, and prostituted herself to pay for her habit. She said that she took all the drugs she could because she knew she would never be alive to see her twenty-first birthday. She smiled and announced that she was now twenty-one. She thanked one staff member after another and one student after another, each for something specific they had contributed to her healing. She said she now felt worthwhile, beautiful and confident. She had learned how to manage the demons in her head. She was beautiful, and it shocked me that she had ever considered anything else, and to the point that she tried to destroy herself. I couldn't help but compare her in my mind to Ashley.

A young man was next. He spoke with a Jersey tough guy accent, was animated as he addressed the room, and his posture was that of some hoodlum walking the streets. He wore a sleeveless white tank top (a wife beater) revealing tattoos covering both his arms and wrapping all the way up around his neck. It seemed like an unusual choice of clothing given the ceremony and the fact that our son had requested that we bring him a suit, but we were looking across such a diverse room that it actually did fit. He was warm and friendly and although his appearance shocked me at first, just as our first impression of this facility had, he too won me over. He had high praise for many of the staff and students and high hopes for what was once a dismal future when he was a drug dealer and an addict. He admitted that he had started his life as a gang member. His life of "gang banging" had led him to do unthinkable things to others and also lead him to a life filled with an abundance of drugs. His drug use had turned into a drug addiction. He knew he needed to change his life or he would end up dead like many of his associates. He spoke candidly about how he needed to forget his old acquaintances and of starting a new life away from the influences that once nearly destroyed him. At the end of his speech, he held his "graduation" plaque proudly in the air to a loud applause.

Our son was last to walk up to the front. As he stood up, we all held hands in anticipation of his speech. He looked each of us in the eyes as he fought tears. He apologized for the damage his addiction had caused. He looked at his mother and me and

102

apologized for more than I can list. He repeated many of the apologies that he had confessed during his many candid phone calls. He looked at his little brother Bryce and apologized for disappointing him and endangering him. He said he was sorry for introducing him to pot so many years before. He asked for his forgiveness and thanked him for his help and encouragement to get through this program. He looked at my mother, his grandmother "Grammy" and apologized for putting her through the same nightmare a second time, as she had been through this with my older brother, Thomas. He looked at Uncle Thomas and thanked him for getting him into a program that saved his life. He thanked staff members and students by name, as he looked them directly in the eyes. He made amends to all of us and he unsuccessfully tried to fight back the tears as he continued. He spoke candidly about all of the lessons he had learned to help him deal with a life without the need for drugs. He talked about how he had learned to deal with the nightmares and guilt he once drowned in drugs. I never thought such words of wisdom and reflection would ever come out of his mouth, but they did. We all sobbed uncontrollably as we could now understand what demons he fought and how our son was back. We could finally understand drug addiction.

A group hug involving our entire family erupted during the ceremony as Brandon finished speaking. I am sure nobody minded the interruption as those in all phases of the program were witnessing the healing of a family. Perhaps it gave them hope as well, and the thought that one day they could hold their loved ones and heal the hurt they had caused. Individual hugs from Brandon followed for each of us, and I thought he would squeeze me to death. When he held his mother, his face was red with emotion and tears. One hug stood out and lasted the longest: When Brandon and his brother hugged, it was intense! It was something for a father and a mother to see, especially given all of the circumstances. Their embrace looked like complete and total forgiveness in a hug. They were whole and all the animosity that had built for years drifted away as they held each other so tightly. They looked like one tangled tree trunk from their feet to their heads. Their arms were wrapped high around each other's shoulders and you could barely see their faces. It was a moment for my wife and me and everyone around us knew how special it was.

Brandon was now over 180 pounds, which filled out his 6'2" frame well. He was working out daily and they were obviously feeding him well. Brandon was physically and mentally a different person. We would later joke that Brandon was so different from the person who we had known as a son these last few years that we should re-name him.

Brandon was accepted to the internship program which would last another three months. First, he returned home for a week to help go through his belongings that we had placed in storage. We ended up throwing away ninety percent of this junk, as he really didn't want much of it anyway. Rummaging through his old belongings was a grim reminder of his former life. Brandon eagerly cleansed himself of almost everything and was resolved to start fresh. His stay at Narconon had also exposed him to a minimalist lifestyle completely unlike his prior existence. He had learned he didn't need "things" to prove anything to anybody. His ex-girlfriend, Tiffanie met us at the storage unit to claim her belongings. She looked about twenty pounds heavier and it was good weight. Tiffanie had been clean and sober since her last relapse in the rehab center. They smiled at each other and commented on their vast physical changes. They knew their life as a couple was over and that they had both gone their separate ways, while both going in the same positive direction— off drugs—despite astronomical odds. The conversation they had was all about sobriety and how wonderful it was to be clean. They both had big smiles and clear eyes and they looked like a couple of healthy young people, and that is exactly what they were.

I also took the opportunity to arrange a meeting at a Starbucks, a reunion of sorts. I had stayed in contact with Officer White by e-mailing him updates on Brandon's progress as a courtesy to him and as a bit of a reward. I thanked him for busting my son. Brandon entered rehab about a month after I did the bust so he wasn't on the streets for long after it all came crashing down. I think without the bust, he could have got killed for stealing from other drug dealers or been captured in a larger bust that he couldn't negotiate his way out of. I knew through our exchange of e-mails that most times he busted someone they ended up repeating the same behavior, eventually ending up in prison or dead. After getting to know the officer I began to realize he was never a bad guy at all as he was just doing a thankless job, often with grim results that left him feeling like his was a fruitless effort to cleanse the streets of dealers and addicts.

When I contacted Officer White and invited him and his Sergeant to meet Brandon and me for coffee, he quickly agreed. The officers were amazed at how healthy Brandon looked and how mature he acted. Brandon greeted them with a handshake that turned into a hug. He thanked them. I think the arrest helped him realize how long the police had been after him and how much they knew about him and that dealers he knew were working for the police. After rehab, when his head was clear, and he knew how close he came to dying or going to prison, I think he respected what the police were doing. By then, several more of his friends had died from an OD or were in rehab or prison. We chatted and the officers said that they called Brandon the "one percent kid" due to his progress through recovery. They also joked about how I was still the talk of the narcotics and uniform officers as this crazy father who went undercover to save his son's ass. It was an odd gathering, but I know the officers enjoyed it and I know they appreciated that their efforts had a positive result on someone.

While we had Brandon home for this brief time we also attended a family wedding. The four of us, Brandon, Bryce, Lisa and myself, drove together several hours north to a coastal town in northern California. We all stayed in the same quaint roadside motel near a popular camping spot called Patrick's Point. It was woodsy and cool and we shared a two-bedroom unit with a common kitchen and a family room with a fireplace. It wasn't much, but it was everything to my wife and me. We took long walks as a family and we talked like we hadn't in years, or possibly ever. We sat by the fireplace and cooked meals together in this tiny motel kitchen. We hiked one day through the forest and climbed a small mountain where we stood together and looked out at the beauty of the nature that surrounded us.

When your children are young, you have many special moments, and they pass by so fast because they are so frequent. People always warn you how fast your children will grow and one day it happens and you realize that you were warned. When your children get old enough to move out of your home, you have very few opportunities to have special family moments and that makes them even more wonderful.

We returned to our home after the trip and we went to bed late that night. I woke that morning before my wife and my sons. I brewed my morning coffee and I walked into Brandon's room. I woke Brandon and I handed him one of the drug tests we still had from our failed attempt to rehabilitate him. It wasn't because I didn't trust him--it was because I did. I believed that every line on that test would indicate he was clean from drugs but I admit that a part of me cringed at the thought of the alternative. He rose quickly from the same bed that he was in the last time I tested him more than six months before. Brandon smiled at me as he walked into the bathroom with a proud and confident look, as only he knew the pending outcome. He finished and sat the testing unit on the counter and he hugged me as if to make up for his last failure. His test was perfect and my son was home and he was clean from the drugs that once consumed him!

The next day Brandon returned to the Narconon facility to start his three months of internship. He would learn how to apply the lessons he learned and many more skills he was yet to be taught. The months went by slowly for him as he worked for no income, as interns do. They fed him and they housed him and they educated him. He had his ups and downs, but he embraced his goal to help others who were afflicted by addiction as he was. He started in detox, which was fitting, as it is exactly where he began. It was a dirty job that we knew all too well. He described how he rubbed the backs of the young men who vomited and comforted them as they reeled in pain from withdrawals. He remembered the video of himself and the comparison was obvious. From there Brandon went through every stage of the program as an intern instead of a student. Brandon even took incoming calls from parents who had children that they were attempting to get into rehab, just as we had called when we were desperate to find our son a place that would help him.

I have also volunteered my time through Narconon to talk to any parent who calls and wants to talk to another parent who has experienced the nightmare they are living. It is hard for me as they tell me their horrific stories of a life we once lived. They tell me it is great to talk to someone who understands what they are experiencing as a parent. Most have no one who can relate so they keep their family secret and they try to figure out what to do just as we did. I don't judge them.

My mother used to say, "I'll always love you, but sometimes I don't like you." I now know exactly what she meant, as I felt that often as a father. Otherwise why would I have done what I did, but for love? Brandon's life was worth saving and as ill prepared as I was to help in many ways, I helped in the only way I could.

Our son now works at Narconon full time. He shares an offsite mobile home with up to six roommates at a time. They have one bathroom but it doesn't seem to bother him in the least. He is happy and he has been drug free for over a year and he lives in a healthy environment. Ironically, Brandon was working the detox center on the day of his one-year anniversary of sobriety. Brandon told us that it suddenly struck him as he sat on the bathroom floor comforting a young man as he convulsed and writhed in pain. Brandon was the young man on the floor twelve months ago, and he had no idea who comforted him that day, but he remembered his compassion well. He had evolved in a short year from the position of a detoxing addict receiving compassion to the position of a former addict providing compassion. Brandon is giving back! Brandon considers the staff and students his second family. We don't see Brandon often because he works in the "boonies" many hours away, but we talk to him almost every night. He usually calls us late after his shift ends around 11 p.m. My wife and I put him on the speaker phone when he calls so we can both share his day with him. He has no car, so he walks about one mile back on the shoulder of the narrow country road in Werner Springs as he talks to us. You can hear the crunching sound of the road's gravel beneath his feet and imagine the gait of his walk from the delay between the sounds. The need for material objects is no longer what he desires and either are the drugs he once craved. We are touched by his compassion, his love and his maturity. We look forward to his call nightly and when we hear sirens, we feel sorrow for the parents whose visions are what ours once were.

Our entire family welcomes our son back and we all realize that no matter how helpless a situation like drug addiction seems we now know that there is help, professional help. Most importantly, there is hope where there is love and there is love where there is family.

Defining Moments

Within any family and throughout the generations there will be many moments that define you as a person. If you are a father or a mother now, there was a day when you were a son or a daughter. Perhaps one day you will become a grandparent. During all of these periods your experiences and certain moments mold you into who you will be. It isn't easy to forget the dark places in your past, but you can either learn from them and become a better person, or repeat the same behavior and have it slowly destroy you.

I make many mistakes as a father, but I have always tried the best I know how. Sometimes no matter what a person does as a parent, children may travel to dangerous places. Some will return from those places unharmed and some may never return. A family can look perfect from the outside but be quite the opposite on the inside. I have lived such a life. I do not know what made me do what I did for my son, but I can only surmise that it was a combination of all of the defining moments in my life that lead me to where I am today.

The beginning ...

Epilogue

Names were changed in this work of narrative non-fiction to protect the innocent and the not-so-innocent.

Steve and Ashley: I would later find out that Steve posted bail and was busted shortly thereafter for robbery and assault as he pistol-whipped and beat his next victim. By the time he went to trial for this bust, he had also been busted again for another drug deal. Steve is now serving five years in prison. The last I heard about Ashley is that she is prostituting herself to support her drug habit.

NARCONON: Information about Narconon is readily available on the Internet; the official site explains the theories of detoxification, based on the work of L. Ron Hubbard.

Brandon: Sadly, as he neared the two-year sobriety mark, Brandon relapsed. I immediately knew just by talking to him over the phone. I wouldn't have noticed the changes in his behavior had I not come to know the new sober Brandon after his treatment at Narconon and his subsequent employment at the facility. Brandon reluctantly agreed to return to Narconon to try to discover "what he had missed," but he didn't go easily. Drug addicts are convinced that they can handle the issue themselves and believing that lie could prove deadly for them. Brandon spent three more months in treatment and is now trying again, living independently in a sober-living environment. Another defining moment for all of us. We hope and pray that Brandon will use the tools he has been taught to navigate through this world where drugs and alcohol are abundant and easy to obtain wherever you live and no matter who you are with. Brandon needs to have the strength and desire to embrace his new healthy body and see the ramifications of destroying himself and his family if he chooses to return to drugs.

Defining Moments

About the Author

Bradley V. DeHaven is a Financial Planner in Sacramento, California, a husband, and a father of two sons, one of whom is a recovering Oxycontin addict.

Brad is pictured here with Brandon in January 2011; Brandon, age 25, is 55 pounds heavier than the 130 pounds his 6'2" body weighed when he entered rehab. Brandon still fights the demons that call to him in his darkest moments. Prescription drug abuse is an epidemic which claims the lives of our youth.

photo by Devin DeHaven, 2011

*I hope that this book and the website **RxDrugAddict.com** can help addicts better understand that they are not just destroying themselves but also their family and friends. I hope they can see that they could have long and productive lives if they chose to feel life instead of numbing it. I also hope this can help people to think about their defining moments and to never give up on their addicted loved ones. Expecting someone to just stop being addicted is as absurd as asking someone to stop having cancer. These addicts need professional help from those who are trained in this field. We are ignorant and ill prepared to help and understand an addict and that ignorance could be deadly. We can only pray that these addicts can overcome their addiction and start living a clean and sober life one day at a time. ~Bradley V. DeHaven*